CISTERCIAN STUDIES SERIES: NUMBER ONE HUNDRED FORTY

Revised Edition

Paphnutius
HISTORIES OF THE MONKS OF UPPER EGYPT
and
THE LIFE OF ONNOPHRIUS

CISTERCIAN STUDIES SERIES: NUMBER ONE HUNDRED FORTY

Revised Edition

HISTORIES OF THE MONKS OF UPPER EGYPT
and
THE LIFE OF ONNOPHRIUS
by
Paphnutius

with

A DISCOURSE ON SAINT ONNOPHRIUS
by
Pisentius of Coptos

Translated, with an Introduction,
by
Tim Vivian

Foreword
by
Jeffrey Burton Russell

Cistercian Publications

A Cistercian Publications title published by Liturgical Press

Cistercian Publications
Editorial Offices
161 Grosvenor Street
Athens, Ohio 45701
www.cistercianpublications.org

© Copyright, Cistercian Publications Inc., 1993
© Translation of *Pisenthius: Discourse on Saint Onnophrius*,
copyright, Cistercian Publications 2000

Translated from E. A. Wallis Budge, *Coptic Texts, IV: Coptic Martyrdoms . . . in the Dialect of Upper Egypt* (London 1914; rpt New York 1977) and *Coptic Texts, V, parts 1 & 2: Miscellaneous Coptic Texts* (London 1915; rpt New York 1977) and from the following manuscripts: British Library, MS Oriental 7029 (*Histories*) and MS Oriental 7027 (*Life of Onnophrius*) and from W, E, Crum, 'Discours de Pisentius sur Saint Onnophrius', Revue de l'Orient Chrétien, 2nd series 10 (20) (191501917) pp. 38–67.

The work of Cistercian Publications is made possible in part by support from Western Michigan University to the Institute of Cistercian Studies.

© 2008 by Order of Saint Benedict, Collegeville, Minnesota. All rights reserved. No part of this book may be reproduced in any form, by print, microfilm, microfiche, mechanical recording, photocopying, translation, or by any other means, known or yet unknown, for any purpose except brief quotations in reviews, without the previous written permission of Liturgical Press, Saint John's Abbey, P.O. Box 7500, Collegeville, Minnesota 56321-7500.

Library of Congress Cataloging-in-Publication Data

Paphnutius, Saint, anchorite, fl. 370.
   [Histories of the monks of upper Egypt. English]
   Histories of the monks of upper Egypt; and, The Life of Onnophrius / by Paphnutius; translated, with an introduction, by Tim Vivian; foreword by Jeffrey Burton Russell.
   p. cm. — (Cistercian studies series; no. 140)
   Translated from the Coptic.
   Includes bibliographical references and index.
   ISBN 0-87907-440-X (alk. paper). — ISBN 0-87907-540-6 (pbk. : alk. paper)
   1. Monasticism and religious orders—Egypt—History. 2. Monasticism and religious orders—History—Early church, ca. 30–600. 3. Onuphrius, Saint, d. ca. 400. 4. Christian saints—Egypt—Biography. 5. Egypt—Church history. I. Paphnutius, Saint, anchorite, fl. 370. Life of St. Onuphrius. English. 1993. II. Vivian, Tim. III. Title: Histories of the monks of upper Egypt. IV. Title: Life of Onnophrius. V. Series.
BX2465.P37   1993
271'.00932—dc20   92-39032
                                                                                           CIP

IN MEMORIAM
THOMAS MERTON

May the memory of Father M. Louis,
who is worthy of praise,
remain with us forever.

TABLE OF CONTENTS

Foreword 9
Preface 13
Introduction 17
    Citizenship with God:
    The Spirituality of Paphnutius' Monks 17
        Mountain and Desert:
            The Geographies of Early Coptic Monasticism
        Eucharist and Synaxis:
            The Celebration of Community
        After God You Are My Salvation:
            The Monk as Holy Man
        The Way of Life
    Paphnutius 42
    The *Histories of the Monks of Upper Egypt* 50
    Aswan and Philae: The Origins of Christianity
    in Upper Egypt 54
    The Manuscripts 69

The *Histories of the Monks of Upper Egypt* 72
    I. Paphnutius Visits Pselusius and the Brethren 73
    II. History of the Bishops of Philae 84
    III. The Life of Abba Aaron 114

The *Life of Onnophrius* 143

Pisentius: *Discourse on Saint Onnophrius*
    Introduction 167
    Text 175

Bibliography 189
Scripture Index 195
Index of Names 199
Index of Subjects 201
Index to Pisentius' *Discourse* 203
Additions and Corrections to the Revised Edition 205

FOREWORD

TIM VIVIAN PRESENTS HERE a new translation of the *Histories of the Monks of Upper Egypt* and the *Life of Onnophrius*, probably by the fourth-century Paphnutius Cephalas. The coptic texts were first edited and translated by E.A.W. Budge in his *Coptic Texts* in 1914–1915, but Budge's translation is now antiquated, and Father Vivian also draws upon some manuscript evidence that Budge did not use. Vivian's translation is smooth and easily accessible to the modern reader, rendering a sensitive, full picture of Paphnutius and his fellow solitaries.

Father Vivian is a reliable, sensitive, and often entertaining guide on an adventure into the deserts of Upper Egypt. Fittingly, he dedicates his book to the truest modern son of the monastic desert, Thomas Merton. He has Merton's intuitive understanding that comes from internal, personal experience, as well as a concrete descriptive power like Peter Brown's, bringing the very shape and smell and silence of the desert before our senses.

The little corner of the fourth-century desert that Father Vivian opens to us is a microcosm of both monasticism and the christian life in general. Vivian's description of the tiny island of Philae in the Nile five miles from Aswan is a sharp picture of life in garrisoned towns at the edge of the Roman Empire where in the fourth century pagans still maintained their temples and shrines along with christian churches.

It was a strange place, the desert of Upper Egypt. In making us familiar with it, Father Vivian does not minimize its strangeness to the modern mind. The monk Isaac, encountering the older monk Abba Aaron standing naked in the solitude with a millstone tied around his neck, reacted to such a sight quite differently than we would: he was blandly unsurprised. But as Paphnutius and his monks are drawn deeper into the strangeness of the desert, they are, oddly, pulled more towards us than away from us.

Drawn deeper into the desert, they are drawn deeper into solitude, deeper into themselves and at the same time deeper into community and deeper into God the ground of being, and thus closer to the ground of being within us, for the depth of being of each of us is as strange and alien, yet hauntingly as familiar, as the desert solitude.

What is this monastic desert? The coptic word *toou* embraces both the greek *eremos*, solitary place, and *oros*, mountain. Physically, it was most often the scrubby, arid lands at the base of the mountains, between the arable Nile and the howling wilderness beyond the mountains. It was poised precariously between civilization and wasteland.

Spiritually and psychologically, it was also a point of balance, of creative tensions and paradoxes. Going out to the barren desert is going in to the fertile source of spiritual life; the stark landscape and sharp shadows of the desert reveal an immediate threat and challenge from Satan yet also the immediate saving power of God; the monks' solitude attracted visitors seeking spiritual direction, then converts, and eventually led to communities of solitaries; withdrawal from the cities produced 'cities' of monks in the desert; commitment to a life of quietism and contemplation entailed a life of active preaching, ministering, and teaching; rejection of the world *against* God (secular, worldly values) meant accepting the world *of* God (the economy of the cosmos that God creates); contemplation opened them to discovery of themselves, which entails both acceptance of oneself and realizing that one's being is utter nothingness unless its base is God.

When understood, these tensions and paradoxes resolve themselves and become identical, a dynamic human analogy of the divine circumincession. The monastic community of solitaries is part of the entire christian community of individual human beings who are in Christ. Aristotle had already understood *politeia*—the way an individual lives his life in community—as arising from the individual's moral life, and early Christianity expanded this secular sense to a spiritual sense of community in Christ.

For the center of monasticism, as of Christianity, is community. As the monks' *politeia* was their common spiritual life, Christianity is and has always been theologically and spiritually a community,

Foreword 11

an organism, a body, the Body of Christ, which exists eternally and embraces in Christ's eternal presence all men and women from every time and place. The center of egyptian monastic life was *synaxis*, the gathering together for worship, and the center of the *synaxis* was the eucharist. As Father Vivian says, 'The community is the body of Christ, and the heart of the community is the eucharist'. Father Vivian understands that the eucharist is a source of power, as Peter Brown observes, but even more the source of nourishment, as Caroline Bynum has seen.

The eucharist is the living heart of the community of monks. And it is the living heart of the communion of 'saints', that is, all those for whom Christ died, is risen, and will come again. The saints never die because the saints live here, now, always, in the undying life that is Christ's body. We are always together with all the saints, in *communion* with them, but sometimes *communication* fails. Sometimes, like family members separated for a while, we lose touch. Tim Vivian puts us back in touch with Paphnutius and Aaron and Onnophrius, from whom we learn and with whom we always pray. I suspect that Father Vivian, like Abba Aaron, would respond: 'Blessed are *you*, Lord, in all *your* works'. But blessed too are they through whom the Lord's light shines.

Jeffrey Burton Russell
University of California
Santa Barbara

PREFACE

A MONG CHRISTIANS OF ALL TRADITIONS, the last twenty years has seen a renewed interest in early christian monasticism. The history, theology, and spirituality of early monasticism, this renewed interest seems to indicate, is relevant to our lives at the end of the twentieth century.

This awakening of interest has brought with it the need for modern translations of the ancient texts from Greek, Latin, Syriac, and Coptic. The histories of Palladius and Theodoret, the lives of Pachomius, Shenoute, and Anthony, and the lives and sayings of the desert fathers (and mothers) have all received fresh english translations in the last twenty-five years, most within the last five to fifteen years. Many of these new translations have been accompanied by helpful introductions to the life of the early monks.[1]

The modern reader can best learn about early monasticism by going to the source—to what the monks themselves had to say. The *Histories of the Monks of Upper Egypt* and the *Life of Onnophrius* take us back to the end of the fourth century and let us see for ourselves at least one small corner of the monastic world.

That world is anchoritic (solitary) rather than cenobitic (large communities under a rule and a master)—although we should be careful not to make those distinctions too sharply or see the two communities as exclusive of one another. The geography of this world is upper Egypt, specifically the area around Aswan and Philae at the southern borders of Egypt. The *Histories* and the *Life* offer both a general introduction to fourth-century monastic

---

[1] I do not use 'nun' for woman this early. The word in Greek is the feminine form of *monachos*, *monachē*. 'Nun' to me implies a medieval nuance.

life and a fascinating glimpse of a localized monasticism with its own distinctiveness and local color.[2] The *Histories* also provide an intriguing account of the origins of Christianity at Philae that seems to be based on local tradition.

In the Introduction, I have tried to lay some groundwork for the general reader. The foundation is, I hope, secured by good scholarship, but I have tried to keep the scholarship to the footnotes. Part One of the Introduction draws the reader's attention to several important topics on the spirituality of Paphnutius' monks and offers some interpretation of and reflection on them. Parts two to four explore the authorship, history, and provenance of the two works by Paphnutius and are necessarily concerned with detail. In the notes I refer the reader to other studies, especially to those in English, and to the recent translations in English mentioned above.

Any selection of topics for the purpose of discussion imposes on the sources an order more apparent than real. In this sense, my presentation of the paphnutian communities is an 'ideal' way of introducing the reader to the major themes of Paphnutius' writings. To mention just two, there was with the monks an ongoing relationship between ascetical practice and charity and hospitality, between the warfare with Satan and the need for contemplation. These relationships often stood in tension—sometimes in conflict. The emphasis of Paphnutius, however, is on the way one comes to God; in my introduction I try to present, as faithfully as possible, the major signposts marking that way.

I wish to thank the Divinity School at Yale University and the Henry R. Luce foundation for a two-year post-doctoral fellowship which allowed me time not only to start this work but also the undistracted silence to continue my reading in Coptic and deepen my study of monasticism, ancient and modern. Abraham Malherbe and James Dittes of the Divinity School directed the program and watched out for its fellows.

Birger Pearson, as always, gave me invaluable assistance. He pored over the problematic passages in the coptic text of the *Histories* and made numerous valuable suggestions; I am grateful

---

[2]For a thorough presentation of fourth-century egyptian monasticism, see Lucien Regnault, *La vie quotienne des pères du desert en Égypte au IV*[e] *siècle* (Paris, 1992). I obtained Regnault's study too late to use it in this book.

for his corrections and emendations. The translation is much the better because of his careful attention. I wish also to thank Bentley Layton and Leo Depuydt at Yale University for their assistance during the early stages of my research. I am grateful to the students in my seminar on early monasticism at Yale Divinity School for the discussions we had about ancient and modern monasticism.

I wish to thank Rowan Greer, Rick Kennedy, Birger Pearson, and Jeffrey Russell for reading the manuscript and offering suggestions from their widely varied perspectives. Rowan Greer also acted as my advisor at Yale Divinity School, and I was grateful for his enthusiasm about my project and for our conversations about this material. Apostolos Athanassakis provided a tentative translation of a greek papyrus letter for this work and also answered several queries I had about unidentified greek loan-words in the coptic texts; I am grateful for his rendering of the greek letter and for his insights into the greek loan-words.

I wish to thank the editors and staff at Cistercian Publications, especially Editorial Director Dr. E. Rozanne Elder, for their assistance in seeing the manuscript through the press. I am grateful to the Reverend Frank Moss, then rector at Saint Andrew's Episcopal Church in Meriden, Connecticut, for his encouragement and support. I wish to thank Stafford and Lynette Betty at California State University, Bakersfield, for help in reading proofs.

Finally, and perhaps most importantly, I wish to thank my wife, Miriam Raub Vivian, who, although herself teaching and helping to raise two children, somehow managed to create enough quiet in the mornings for me to work on this translation of Paphnutius.

I have compared my translation at every point with the one made by E.A. Wallis Budge early in this century. Budge's translation is now archaic, and it contains a number of errors. I have not hesitated in following Budge at numerous points, however, or in borrowing from his rendering felicitous words or phrasings. Budge was a great scholar, and all students of egyptian life and literature are in his debt. It was while reading his collection of *Coptic Texts* that I first came upon Paphnutius and realized that he deserved a wider audience. Budge was the first to recognize the importance of Paphnutius' *Histories*, and it is my hope that the present translation continues his great work.

In the translation I have attempted to be idiomatic without being slangy. We should remember that the ancient monks were people, not holy artifacts. We should also remember that all with them was not utter seriousness.

The dedication is to the monk and desert father whose spirit—and spirit of play—accompanied me during the writing of this work and whose writings made of my urban back porch in New Haven a true desert hermitage.

Tim Vivian

Advent, 1992
Bakersfield, California

INTRODUCTION

CITIZENSHIP WITH GOD: THE
SPIRITUALITY OF PAPHNUTIUS' MONKS

IN THE CLASSICAL GREEK WORLD and later in the hellenistic period, a person was a citizen of a *polis* or city. *Politeia* meant 'citizenship' and 'the daily life of a citizen'. It could also signify 'a body of citizens', or 'a corporate body or an association'.[1]

The word 'politeia' occurs in the title of the *Life of Onnophrius*: 'The Life [*bios*] and Ascetic Practice [*politeia*] of our Holy Father Abba Onnophrius'. The *Life of Onnophrius*, then, sets out to tell not just the 'life' of the saint, but something more. *Politeia* is not opposed to *bios*; it is at once part of a life and at the same time something in addition to a 'life'. One might call it the heart or soul of life.

In patristic Greek, the original political meaning of 'politeia', the daily life of a citizen, came to have a moral connotation: 'way of life, conduct, behavior'. A religious way of life then came to mean 'ascetic practice' or 'an act of religious behavior'. The verb *politeuein* meant 'to live as a member of a community, share a particular mode of life'.[2]

In the *Histories of the Monks of Upper Egypt* and the *Life of Onnophrius*, *politeia* (and its cognate verb *politeuein*) has all of the meanings listed in the preceding paragraph. It can be translated

---

[1] Henry George Liddell and Robert Scott, rev. by Henry Stuart Jones, *A Greek-English Lexicon* (Oxford: Clarendon Press, 1968) 1434.
[2] G.W.H. Lampe, ed., *A Patristic Greek Lexicon* (Oxford: Clarendon Press, 1978) 1113A (F–G).

simply 'lives', but in a special sense: 'to everyone in the desert who lives [*politeue*] there on account of God and sees no human being the angel comes and gives the eucharist and comforts them' (*Onnophrius*, par. 17). Monks are understood to be citizens of the desert. Desert citizenship has two requisites: the monk lives in the desert on account of God, and he or she has withdrawn from life in the 'world' to live more closely with God. A monk is a citizen *of* God and *with* God.

Because of this citizenship, a monk practices *politeia* as a strict way of life (*Histories*, par. 17). In the *Life of Onnophrius*, such a way of life when practised by 'the holy ones' is worthy of emulation (par. 34). An ascetic life produces ascetic practice, another meaning of *politeia*: Matthew, although he was 'very learned and had been instructed in the writings of holy scripture', because of his humility 'could never be persuaded to speak about any saying' (*Histories*, par.16). Serapamon's *politeia* is to sacrifice his handiwork for others and for the good of the community. He 'continued in this act of love until the day of his perfection' (par. 15). Citizenship with God on earth leads to eternal citizenship with the saints in heaven.

Mountain and Desert: The Geographies of Early Coptic Monasticism

Monasticism, then as now, is a spirituality of the desert. A monk does not enter the desert so much to escape the world as to encounter God and wage war on Satan.[3] As Thomas Merton observed many times, the desert does not have to be a geographical reality; it must, however, be a spiritual reality.[4] For egyptian monks of the fourth century, the desert was a geographical reality—both

---

[3] On the vast literature of early monasticism, see Derwas J. Chitty, *The Desert a City* (Crestwood, New York, n.d.) pp. 216–221, and Tim Vivian, 'Reading The Saints: Early Monastic Sources Available in English', *Cistercian Studies Quarterly* 28/1 (1993). On the spirituality, see Louis Bouyer, *A History of Christian Spirituality*, 1, *The Spirituality of the New Testament and the Fathers* (London-New York, 1963); Kenneth Leech, *Experiencing God: Theology as Spirituality* (San Francisco, 1985) 127–61; Thomas Merton, *The Wisdom of the Desert* (New York, 1960) 3–24, and *The Climate of Monastic Prayer* (Spencer, 1969, Kalamazoo, 1981) 121–9.

[4] See e.g. Thomas Merton, *The Silent Life* (New York, 1989) pp. 60 and 146. For introductions to Thomas Merton on monasticism, see *Contemplation in a World of Action* (New York, 1973) and *The Monastic Journey* (New York, 1978).

in place and in memory. In place because they lived outside the immediate area watered by the Nile; in memory because the sacred scriptures told them that the people of Israel had wandered in the desert; Elijah, Elisha, and John the Baptist had prophesied in the desert; their Lord and Saviour after his baptism had been driven by the Spirit into the desert.

In Coptic, the word *toou* signifies both mountain and desert (in Greek, respectively, *oros* and *erēmos*), and can mean any land outside of the immediate vicinity of the Nile:

> The Egyptian desert ends abruptly in an escarpment overlooking the flat valley floor of the Nile. *Oros* is therefore barren, uncultivated land, not necessarily rising to any height, as against the irrigated zone of the valley and delta.[5]

In the monastic literature, 'mountain' and 'desert' have both a geographical and a religious sense.[6]

Geographical

(1) 'Open' desert or 'true' desert: the large desert plateaux which overhang the Nile valley.[7]

(2) The desert or hilly escarpment: the neighboring or bordering desert. In the papyri this seems to be a more frequent use of the word.[8]

For a good recent study on desert spirituality, see Andrew Louth, *The Wilderness of God* (London, 1991).

[5] Norman Russell, tr., *The Lives of the Desert Fathers* (Kalamazoo, Michigan-London-Oxford, 1981) p. 125 n.12.

[6] The discussion on pp. 19–20 is taken from Russell, p. 125 n.12, and H. Cadell and R. Rémondon, 'Sens et emplois de τὸ ὄρος dans les documents papyrologiques,' *Revue des études grecques* 80 (1967) 343–49. See also Hugh G. Evelyn White, *The Monasteries of the Wâdi 'N Natrûn* (New York, 1926–33 [repr. 1973]) 2:21–22.

[7] Cadell and Rémondon, 343. In modern Egypt, at least in the early part of this century, 'the steep, sometimes almost precipitous ascent to the high-desert plateau' is called 'the mountain'. See Winifred S. Blackman, *The Fellāhīn of Upper Egypt: Their Religious, Social, and Industrial Life To-day, with Special Reference to Survivals from Ancient Times* (London, 1927) p. 23.

[8] Cadell and Rémondon, 343.

(3) 'The approach to the desert': the strip of land between the alluvial plain and the escarpment, marking the extreme limits of cultivated—and therefore inhabited—land.[9] This is where numerous monasteries were situated: Apollo 'had hermitages under him in the desert at the foot of the mountain. . . .'[10]

Religious

(1) The word *oros* can mean a monastery: the '*monasterion* of Abba Agenios' is interchanged with the '*oros* of Abba Agenios'.[11] Abû Ṣâliḥ, in the twelfth century, described several 'mountains' in the vicinity of Aswan with churches and monasteries on them:

> [There is also] a ruined church of the glorious angel Michael outside Ûswan [sic], to the east, upon the mountain; and the church of the saint and glorious martyr George. [There is also] a monastery of the saint Abû Hadrî on the mountain on the west; and it is inhabited by monks. The monastery of Saint Anthony is built of stone. It possessed several gardens, but the Arabs seized them and wrecked the monastery.[12]

(2) *Oros* can signify not only a monastery, but also an area where there is a concentration of monasteries:[13] 'The Monasteries and hermitages among the West Theban rocks are dignified now and then by the general name of "the Holy Hill," borrowed, if not directly from the Psalter, perhaps from Sinai; or from the

---

[9]Cadell and Rémondon, 343.
[10]*Historia Monachorum* 8.2; Russell, p. 70. Abba Or 'had spent much time practicing the ascetic life, as a solitary in the further desert (καθ' ἑαυτὸν ἐν τῇ ἐρήμῳ ἀσκήσας τῇ πορρώτερα). Afterwards he organized the hermitages in the nearer desert (ἐν τῇ πλησίον ἐρήμῳ), and planted a marsh with his own hands. . . . The fathers who lived near him said to us concerning him: "There was not a single green shoot here before the father came out of the desert"'. For the greek text, see A.-J. Festugière, ed., *Historia Monachorum in Aegypto, Subsidia Hagiographica* n. 34 (Brussels, 1961) pp. 35–6.
[11]Caddell and Rémondon, 347; they give examples from the papyri.
[12]B.T.A. Evetts and Alfred J. Butler, *The Churches and Monasteries of Egypt and Some Neighbouring Countries* (Oxford, 1895, repr. London, 1969) p. 277.
[13]Caddell and Rémondon, 347.

Mount of Olives: the will of bishop Abraham speaks of the θεῖον ὄρος Μεμνονίων, another deed of "the holy hill of the *castrum* of Jême".'[14]

(3) In the *Life of Pachomius*, a mountain can be a place where solitaries gather; it is an area where a group of anchorites is loosely gathered around a spiritual master. Abba Palamon, a 'father and comforter' (and 'novice master' to the young Pachomius), 'was in contact with all those who had settled on that mountain'.[15]

(4) By extension, 'mountain' can even suggest the place where solitaries are laid to rest: after Abba Palamon's death, 'they offered the Eucharist for him, and they brought him to the mountain at a little distance from his cell. They buried him and prayed for him; then each one returned to his cell. . . .'[16] When Pachomius died, 'all night long they kept vigil about him with reading and prayers. Then his body was prepared and carried away to the mountain in like manner with psalms and buried. When they had come down, Theodore and three other brothers transferred it to another place, where it is to this day'.[17]

The desert was a fearful place. The *Historia Monachorum* reports that Elias lived

> in the desert (ἐρήμῳ) of Antinoe. . . . He was famous for having spent seventy years in the terrible desert (ἐν τῇ φοβερᾷ ἐρήμῳ). No description can do justice to that rugged desert (ἔρημον) in the mountain (ἐν τῷ ὄρει) where [he] had his hermitage, never coming down to the inhabited region (οἰκουμένην). The path which one took to go to him was so narrow that those who pressed on could only just follow its track with rough crags towering on either side. He had his seat

---

[14]H.E. Winlock and W.E. Crum, *The Monastery of Epiphanius at Thebes* (New York, 1926) 1:127.

[15]*Vita Pachomii* 14 (Veilleux, p. 37) and 16 (p. 38). The spiritual master taught by word and example: 'On hearing these terrifying words from their father Apa Palamon, the brothers were powerfully moved to keep themselves with great courage in the future and to save themselves. Their dread was greater still at contemplating his example, for he bore in his flesh at all times the Cross of Christ'.

[16]*Vita Pachomii* 18 (Veilleux, p. 40); see also *The First Greek Life* [G 1] 32 (Veilleux, p. 320).

[17]G 1: 116; Veilleux, p. 380.

under a rock in a cave, so that even the sight of him was very impressive.[18]

Modern accounts of the desert help us appreciate the courage of Elias, Anthony, and the other mothers and fathers of the desert:

> The vast solitudes of the desert are terrifying to the country folk, most of whom, up to the present day, cannot be induced to traverse even the lower fringes of those wastes after sunset. Fear of hyenas, and, still more, of *'afārīt* [demons], forbids any man to venture beyond the cultivation at night. The ordinary peasant, unless he is obliged to remain in the fields either to protect his crops or to watch over his sheep and goats, returns to his village before sunset, remaining there until just before the dawn of the following day.[19]

Separated from the inhabited, arable world, the desert, as the *Life of Anthony* and subsequent monastic literature amply show, was the place where a person confronted demons—and the demons of the human heart. It was a city outside the city, and in this place a person learned true citizenship with God. Such citizenship could be best lived by practising *ascesis*, an ascetic way of life: by stripping away the layers of extra clothing laid on one by the world, a person could stand naked before God—as some anchorites, such as Onnophrius, quite literally did.[20] This ascesis could be practised in the city, but most monks believed it could be done better in the desert. Dual citizenship, they usually insisted, was not easy—if it was possible at all.[21]

---

[18]*Historia Monachorum* 7.1; Russell, p. 69.
[19]Blackman, p. 21.
[20]Changing clothes could symbolize a change of life. See Bernard Flusin and Joseph Paramelle, 'De Syncletica in deserto Iordanis', *Analecta Bollandiana* 100 (1982) 313–14, and Tim Vivian, 'Syncletica: A Sixth-century Female Anchorite', *Vox Benedictina* (forthcoming).
[21]An intermediary 'order' of monks between the anchorites and cenobites, the *apotaktikoi*, apparently stayed close to home; they dwelt in the towns and cities of fourth- and fifth-century Egypt and Palestine. For a fascinating glimpse of these *monachoi*, see E.A. Judge, 'The Earliest Use of Monachos for "Monk" (P. Coll. Youtie 77) and the Origins of Monasticism', *Jahrbuch für Antike und Christentum* 20 (1977) 72–89. Saint Jerome did not approve of them (p. 79): 'apud hos affecta sunt omnia: . . . visitatio virginum, detractio clericorum, et si

Within this understanding, then, the word 'desert' takes on two additional levels of meaning: the spiritual and the mystical. Not only was the desert a religious *place*, it signified a spiritual *way of being*. It was where one could live most closely with God and learn the virtues of a christian life. As John of Lycopolis told his disciples:

> And so, my children, first of all let us discipline ourselves to attain humility, since this is the essential foundation of all virtues. At the same time, the remoter desert (ἡ μακρότερα ἔρημος) is also profitable to us for the practice of ascesis. For example, there was another monk who had settled in the further desert (τὴν πορρωτέρω ἔρημον) and had practiced the virtues for many years.[22]

The desert stood in opposition to the *oikoumenē*, the inhabited world, not because the world was necessarily a bad place but because the desert was a better place to be in close relationship with God (see the story of Abba Elias above, pp. 21–22). Finally, the concept of desert took on a mystical meaning: the desert came to represent the holy, the pure, the non-'world'. This could be— and often was—understood in a dualistic sense wherein the world was evil and the desert good. But that understanding is not as common in early monastic literature as is popularly believed.[23] The desert was where one could be perfected in God.

This mystical meaning does not by any means suggest that the importance and reality of place was forgotten. The harsh reality of life in the egyptian desert would not allow such a 'spiritualization'! A mystical understanding of the desert was similar to a mystical understanding of Scripture. Patristic biblical exegesis, as practised for example by Origen, did not deny the literal reality of events in the Bible; it sought to find in them deeper meanings. The same was true of the desert.

---

quando festior dies venerit, saturantur ad vomitum.' ('Among them everything is done for effect: they pay visits to virgins, belittle the clergy, and, whenever a feast day comes around, eat so much they throw up.') On Mount Athos there has historically been a similar tension between the anchorites and cenobites on the one hand and the idiorrhythmic monks on the other.

[22]*Historia Monachorum* 1.44–45; Russell, p. 59. For the greek text, see Festugière, p. 26.

[23]See Thomas Merton's *The Wisdom of the Desert*.

In the *Historia Monachorum*, when a certain Abba Paphnutius wishes to see examples of perfection (in whose image, he fancies, his own virtues are brilliantly reflected), he is humbled by an angel who tells him he is like three worldlings who still have a great deal to learn. Each believes he leads a godly life, but that is not enough: to be perfect each must abandon the wealth and prestige of the world and go into the wilderness of self-denial and absolute surrender to God. Paphnutius becomes their spiritual leader and guides each one into the wilderness where he is perfected. Before Paphnutius' own perfection, however, he must learn from the angel that these 'worldly' people have in turn acted as spiritual directors for him: they have shown the way to God. His pride had prevented him from seeing this; he had practiced *ascesis* for years, and *ascesis* had become a source of pride. He had to unlearn his spiritual hubris and study humility before he could die in the Lord.[24]

Paphnutius had already lived in the desert; the desert he now discovered was the desert of his own soul. It must not have been an easy lesson. Paphnutius tells the first of the three worldlings, a flute player, that he must follow him into the 'desert'; he tells the village leader and the merchant that they must follow him into the 'mountain'. Desert and mountain have the same meaning here, a meaning both geographical and mystical. There is no doubt that the three go out into the actual desert; at the same time, however, no further geography is mentioned. Details are not important. We are in a mystical landscape, where meaning is found not in heat and cold and the coarseness of terrain but in the interior geography of the human soul and its relationship with God.

The little-known but important story of Abba Pambo well illustrates the mystical meaning of the desert. In a vision, Pambo is told to find a certain anchorite, a holy man, so he journeys into the desert to meet him. Before he can find the holy man, though, Pambo comes upon two other monks. Each tells him that he is not the sought-after holy man, so Pambo asks each if there is anyone beyond him in the desert. Each monk says, 'Yes, there is. There is one whose sandal straps no one is fit to untie'. So Pambo each time journeys deeper into the desert. It becomes clear (to the reader, if not immediately to Pambo) that Pambo's journey

---

[24] *Historia Monachorum* 14.15; Russell, pp. 95–98.

cannot be measured in miles: one does not get holier the further one goes into the desert. The story cares little for geographical detail. Pambo is on a spiritual journey, into himself and into God, a journey on which he must shake off his naive presuppositions and learn about God in the heart of the incarnation.[25]

In the *Histories of the Monks of Upper Egypt* and the *Life of Onnophrius*, mountain and desert carry these four levels of meaning: geographical, religious, spiritual, and mystical. The four overlap, and one should not see them as being set in a hierarchy where the spiritual and mystical are more important than the geographical and religious (the narrators of both stories, as well as Abba Pambo, return to their monasteries). Nor should one make the four senses too easily divisible. They coinhere.

Abba Isaac, in the third section of the *Histories*, desires to sit at the feet of the holy man Abba Aaron, and goes into the desert to find him. He locates the monk's home, but the old anchorite is not there. Isaac must go still further into the desert. He finds Aaron, stays with him, and is made a monk. But after a week Aaron leaves Isaac and goes off alone, like Jesus, to pray. Left by himself, Isaac is immediately assaulted by demons and hurries off once again into the desert to find his spiritual father. The old man asks his disciple why he has come and the latter replies, 'The Nubians have been tormenting me and I've come to tell you!' Abba Aaron smiles and gently chides Isaac, 'Truly they are invisible Nubians, my son' (pars. 93–4).

In this story the desert is a place (it *is* hot), and it is a place of ascesis (each time Isaac finds Aaron the latter is practising severe ascetical exercises). But it is also a place of discovery. It is where the disciple learns about monastic practice, and it is where he discovers the depths of his own fears.

Onnophrius, too, journeys into the desert to find a spiritual master. When Onnophrius finds him, his teacher takes him further into the desert where the disciple learns the monastic life. When Paphnutius hears Onnophrius' story, he, like Pambo, can only wonder incredulously about such a life. Didn't Onnophrius suffer unbearably from the inhospitable weather? Onnophrius answers

---

[25]See Tim Vivian, 'Journeying into God: The Story of Abba Pambo', *Cistercian Studies Quarterly* 26:2 (1991). For the coptic text, see Budge, IV:128–36; English translation, 381–9.

that at first he did, but the Lord, seeing his endurance, made the palm trees and plants nourish him and the holy angels serve him daily with food. Onnophrius, quoting Matthew 6:31–33, tells Paphnutius that if you do the will of God, God will care for you: ' "Take no care for what you will eat or what you will drink or what you will clothe yourself with. Your father in heaven knows what you need without your asking him. Instead, seek his kingdom and his righteousness and these things will be added unto you" ' (par. 16).

The monastic desert, paradoxically, is a place of sustenance and provision. Angels minister to the monks, and date-palms produce fruit year around (*Onnophrius* par. 16). There are unexplainable instances where fruit is incredibly abundant and visions are granted (*Onnophrius* pars. 28–9). Miracles and visions serve to underscore the reality of the desert. As Abba Onnophrius tells Paphnutius: 'I live in the desert on account of my sins' (par. 10). But the desert is also where one flees from sin (*Onnophrius* pars. 6–7). The desert is a city, but it is more. The desert is the way human beings live in the world. It is also a *cosmos*, a spiritual and mystical universe which, for the monks, is made in the image of heaven. As Thomas Merton exclaimed,

> And the deep ferns sing this epithalame:
> "Go up, go up! this desert is the door of heaven!
> And it shall prove your frail soul's miracle!
> Climb the safe mountain,
>
> Disarm your labored flesh, and taste the treasures
>   of these silences
> In the high coral hermitage,
> While the clean winds bemuse you in the
>   clefted rock;..."[26]

Eucharist and Synaxis: The Celebration of Community

There is a lingering misconception that monasticism, ancient and modern, is individualistic in its piety, that monks avoid at all

---

[26]From 'The Landfall', *Selected Poems* (New York, 1967) p. 73.

costs contact with other people and the world. The truth is that monasticism, even eremitic, anchoritic monasticism, is essentially communal. The community is the body of Christ, and the heart of the community is the eucharist. Louis Bouyer has described the laura founded near Jerusalem by Saint Saba in the fifth century as 'a group of solitaries who gather every Saturday and Sunday for services and spiritual reunions around a master, in a vast grotto or some central buildings'.[27] Ancient monasticism is fundamentally defined by *coming together* as a group, as a community, with a spiritual master, for the purpose of worshiping God.

This 'coming together' in early monasticism was the *synaxis*, 'a gathering, assembly for public worship and instruction'. Specifically, 'synaxis' often means 'to come together to share in the eucharist'.[28] The frequency of the eucharistic *synaxis* varied among the monks, from infrequent to daily. In Egypt the common practice in the fourth and fifth centuries was to come together for the eucharist on Saturday and Sunday (the Sabbath and the Lord's day).[29]

In early monasticism the eucharist was not set off from the activities of day-to-day life; it was often a part of a monastic community's hospitality to strangers. Being welcomed to a community would often include a greeting, the washing of feet, the eucharist, and a meal.[30] Hospitality was a cardinal virtue among the monks of the desert, an ordinance given them by Christ's

---

[27]Bouyer, *History*, 1:330.

[28]Lampe, p. 1302A. 'Synaxis' has a wide range of meaning. See Lampe, and Russell, p. 133, n.2. 'Synaxis' can mean the divine office or any meeting in church, sometimes even the church itself. It can also mean 'a collection of prayers'. See further Armand Veilleux, *La liturgie dans le cénobitisme Pachômien au quatrième siècle* (Rome, 1968) pp. 293–4. Veilleux notes, *Pachomian Koinonia* 1:269, par 18, n.2, that in the pachomian coptic sources the usual term for eucharist is *prosphora*. On the eucharistic practice of early egyptian monks, especially of pachomian cenobitic monasticism, see Veilleux, *La liturgie*, pp. 226–248.

[29]Veilleux, *Pachomian Koinonia*, 1:271, par. 25, n.4, gives examples. He notes, p. 233, that Pachomius followed the general practice of his time in celebrating the eucharist on Saturday and Sunday. On the frequency of communion, see Benedicta Ward's introduction in Russell, p. 26. She observes that the monks of Nitria came together on Saturday and Sunday. See also Veilleux, *La liturgie*, pp. 233–41. On daily communion, see Chadwick, *John Cassian*, p. 69. According to Chadwick, 'there are faint traces of a practice in the Egyptian desert of taking the reserved Sacrament back to the cell and partaking there'.

[30]Ward, in Russell, p. 26.

example. When they made the eucharist part of hospitality, they were acknowledging the importance of both and the value each gave to the other.

The eucharist and *synaxis* lay at the center of early monastic praxis, theology, and spirituality. According to the *Historia Monachorum*, the monks of Nitria

> inhabit a desert place and have their cells some distance from each other, so that no one should be recognized from afar by another, or be seen easily, or hear another's voice. On the contrary, they live in profound silence, each monk isolated on his own. They come together in the churches only on Saturdays and Sundays, and meet one another. Many of them who die in their cells are often not found for four days, because they do not see each other except at the *Synaxis*. Some of them, living as they do far apart from each other, travel three or four miles to the *Synaxis*.[31]

No monk, no matter how pious or how profoundly deep in solitude, was to miss the eucharist.

> We saw a priest there called Piammonas, a holy and very humble man who frequently saw visions. Once when he was celebrating the Eucharist he saw an angel standing to the right of the altar. The angel was noting the brethren who came up for Communion and writing down their names in a book. As for those who were not present at the Synaxis, he saw their names erased. And in fact thirteen days later these died.[32]

Abba John, the *Historia Monachorum* records, 'spent his time in the desert wandering about and eating plants. But on Sundays he was always at the same place to receive Communion'.[33]

The eucharist requires a priest, and many monastic communities—including, it seems, those in the *Life of Onnophrius*—had no clergy. According to one story, Abba Helle goes to see some monks and ask them why they have not celebrated the *synaxis*

---

[31]Russell, p. 106.
[32]Russell, p. 116.
[33]Russell, p. 94.

that day. They reply that it was because the priest had not come from the other side of the river. Abba Helle investigates and finds out that the priest is afraid to come because of a crocodile in that part of the river 'which had devoured many people'. Helle tames the beast and tells the priest to climb aboard. The priest declines. Whether or not he changed his mind is not recorded.[34]

The *Life of Onnophrius* contains a striking passage where four monks in the remote desert are able to participate in the eucharist without the benefit of a priest. Paphnutius asks the four, 'Where do you gather for the eucharist?' They say to him,

> We assemble right here for that purpose, and on every Sabbath an angel of God comes and gives us communion on the Sabbath and on the Lord's day. . . . On the seventh day of the week an angel of the Lord will give communion to us and to you together, and the person who receives communion from the hand of that angel will be washed clean from all sin and the Adversary will in no way have power over him (par. 32).[35]

The eucharist freed the monk from sin and gave him power. The desert anchorite had a very clear-headed and sensible understanding of evil: evil exists, and manifests itself in dramatic ways in people's lives. Evil has power, even if that power is usually illusory or fleeting. God, too, has power, greater power than the Devil, and the eucharist—along with ascesis, prayer, hospitality, and works of love—is a channel, perhaps the greatest channel, of God's power.

Yet we would better understand the eucharist in terms of nourishment and sustenance than of power. The eucharist is bread and wine. Another 'miracle' shows Paphnutius that in the monks' lives the power of God does not restrict itself to the eucharist and great signs and wonders, but extends itself to the very act of eating and sharing a meal, the foundation of eucharist and community. Paphnutius meets four monks and they ask him to eat with them:

> Now while we were talking together, five loaves of bread were brought in, warm and fresh as though

---

[34]Russell, pp. 90–1.
[35]Veilleux, *La liturgie*, p. 228, n.9, says, with understatement, that this is 'an interesting example'. See par. 11 of the *Life of Onnophrius* for a similar account.

straight from the oven; furthermore, in quick succession other dishes were brought in. We sat down and ate together and he said to me, 'See, we have been here six years, and four loaves of bread have been allotted to us each day, and these came to us from God. Now since you have come to us today, look, a fifth loaf has been brought for you. We have never known where they come from, but when we come in we find them sitting here.[36]

The eucharist is a mystery. The monks whom Paphnutius meets in the desert understand this. But mystery is not something separated off and kept in hiding; mystery, like bread, is daily and sacramental. 'Eucharist' and 'synaxis' occur, surprisingly, only a few times in the *Histories of the Monks of Upper Egypt*. Yet, if the story of the founding of the see of Philae has any historical reliability, Christianity was established there because of the need for the eucharist (see pars. 29–30). And if the story is not historically true, it nevertheless reflects the importance of the eucharist in the lives of the Christians who told it and handed it on to Paphnutius. To them the eucharist was the cornerstone of the Church at Philae.

After God You Are My Salvation: The Monk as Holy Man

At the end of the fourth century, the *Historia Monachorum* recorded that the monks of upper Egypt 'raise the dead and walk on the water just like Peter. And all that the Saviour did through the saints, he does in our times through these monks'.[37] Jesus performed miracles, and the Acts of the Apostles records how his disciples continued to heal in his name. The monks of Egypt believed they were following their Master and the apostles and saints before them when they performed miracles, healed the sick, and raised the dead.

An especially wise and saintly monk, usually (but not always) in old age, came to be regarded as a holy man. As a person known for

---

[36] *Life of Onnophrius*, par. 26. Bread from heaven is a common occurence in the *Historia Monachorum*. See, e.g., 1.47 (John of Lycopolis); Russell, p. 59.
[37] *Historia Monachorum*, Epilogue; Russell, p. 118.

his sanctity and healing powers, he attracted disciples who wished to sit at his feet and learn from him. In a sense, such a christian holy man merely replaced the non-christian priest in his area and, in later centuries, came to have more and more social and political power.[38] Holy men—and women—were a vital part of the life of their village. One twentieth-century holy woman may give us a clearer picture of her ancient predecessors:

> In one of the provinces in Upper Egypt, close to the desert hills, lived the *sheikeh* [holy woman] Sulūh. This woman had, during her lifetime, a great reputation for holiness, and people flocked to her, in times of difficulty, from all quarters. Her skin was very dark from constant exposure to the sun, and her head, on which she wore no veil, was covered with a crop of hair, thick and long like the wool of a sheep; from beneath her brows peered dark, sharp-looking eyes. Her clothes were scanty, consisting merely of a piece of linen rag and a sort of coat. She remained out in the desert solitude all day, and at night, so I was told, slept alone 'in the mountain'.[39]

One of Sulūh's ancient counterparts, Apollo, a monk near Hermopolis in the Thebaid, destroyed a local idol that used to 'ensure the flooding of the Nile'.[40] The farmers would still need the Nile to flood to irrigate their land and, in times of distress, would still need divine help and assurance. Whether they were Christians or not, if there was a powerful man of God in the area, they went to him. Such a person was Abba Aaron, whose life and deeds occupy the final third of Paphnutius' *Histories*.

One day some men come to Abba Aaron, 'terrified because the proper time for the rising of the waters had passed. And they continued to weep [and beg the holy man. He had] compassion [on them and prayed to God,] saying, "God, do not forsake the

---

[38]The seminal discussion of the holy man in late antiquity is Peter Brown's 'The Rise and Function of the Holy Man in Late Antiquity,' *Journal of Roman Studies* 61 (1971) 80–101. Brown is concerned mostly with syrian monks at a later period.
[39]Blackman, pp. 246–7.
[40]*Historia Monachorum* 8.24–29; Russell, pp. 73–4.

work of your hands, man and beast. For indeed you created us all from your blood and you deigned to come into the world"'. Aaron preaches a short sermon on mercy and dismisses the men in peace, saying, 'God will make the river fill with water, and he will bring it to its proper level. Do not be afraid, and do not be unbelieving'. Aaron then goes down to the river and prays to God:

> Lord, you are the same yesterday, and today, and forever. It was you who burst open the rock and water flowed forth and you gave it to the people to drink. And when Samson was thirsty you caused the jawbone of an ass to bring forth water which quenched his thirst. Therefore, I entreat you today to send the river's water over the entire land so the poor among your people have enough food and bless you and your holy name.

The river rises, and 'there was abundance and plenty that year through the prayers of the holy man, as it is written, "The prayer of a righteous man is powerful and effective"' (pars. 132–5).

Is what Aaron does a miracle, or is it 'the prayer of a righteous man,' 'powerful and effective'?[41] The question is undoubtedly a modern one. Phrased in this 'either/or' manner, it falsely separates the miracle from the life of the holy man. It divides the singular act from the ongoing activity of prayer and contemplation which was the monk's life (see 'The Way of Life' below, pp. 37–41).

The holy man understood that contemplation and action went together. 'Action' could be something as simple as mat-weaving, disposing one to contemplation. Abba Aaron plaited rope and sewed burial shrouds; Gandhi sat at the spinning wheel. Action could also be pastoral; then it took on greater social importance as the holy man became community healer and reconciler. Macedonius, the first bishop of Philae, is appealed to by nubian camel herders to settle their dispute;[42] Abba Aaron causes the waters of the Nile to rise. Actions such as these should be seen in their proper context: Macedonius at first declines to hear the 'case' of the Nubians, but when he reads in the lectionary, 'Blessed are

---

[41] For a discussion of the role of miracles in the lives of the monks, see Benedicta Ward's introduction in Russell, pp. 39–45.

[42] For a similar modern story, see p. 92 below.

the peacemakers, for they shall be called children of God', he goes down to them; before Aaron performs his miracle, he speaks about justice and mercy to those who have come to him.

As far back as Saint Anthony—in other words, at the beginning of monasticism—monastic spirituality understood contemplation and action as a seamless garment which the monk wove with his or her life. Through Anthony, 'the Lord healed many persons suffering in their bodies, and purified others of demons. Anthony had received from God the grace of consoling the afflicted, of reconciling men at odds with one another. He told them to esteem nothing in the world more than the love of Christ'.[43] The monastic life aimed not at building up of the self but, through the love of Christ, at healing the world.

The life of Abba Aaron, as told by Isaac to Paphnutius, is a paradigm of this understanding. Isaac heard a 'report' about Aaron: he was 'living the monastic life in a place called "the valley", and was performing many cures for all those who were sick' (par. 90). In this sentence, as in Aaron's life, the monastic life and healing are joined together. In his account of Aaron's life, Isaac gives much more space to the holy man's miracles of healing and reconciliation than to his feats of asceticism and self-denial (though the latter are certainly present). It is not an exaggeration to say that Aaron's miracles and acts of healing *are* his *politeia*, his way of life: they arise naturally and simply from his life of prayer, from the way he is present to God, God's grace, and God's world.

Death and resurrection lie at the heart of Abba Aaron's ministry, and thus the old man's *politeia* is a true *imitatio Christi*. Isaac, playing Elisha to Aaron's Elijah, relates the first miracle he saw: one day while a Nubian and his son were fishing, a crocodile seized the boy and dragged him into the river. The father, in distress, cut himself badly while running wildly up a mountain. Aaron healed the father and restored the boy, dragged underwater by the crocodile, through prayer.

In the next miracle related by Isaac, a fisherman's son gets tangled in a fishing net and supposedly drowns. But because of Abba Aaron's prayers the child while underwater sees a vision of light and is miraculously freed from the net: 'It happened that

---

[43] *Life of Anthony* 14.

when I got tangled up in the net and was about to lose my last breath, I looked and saw a man of light. He took me by the hand and freed me from the net and brought me up into the boat. And suddenly I no longer saw him' (par. 102).

The images of water, of death and rebirth, of baptism, are central to these stories. In several other stories, Abba Aaron raises the dead by sprinkling water which he has blessed: a vineyard worker falls from a tree and seems to be dead, but is restored when sprinkled with holy water (pars. 103–4), and a rich man has his sight restored when he washes his face with water blessed by Abba Aaron (par. 115). In a variation on this theme, a stillborn child is made alive when sprinkled with earth taken from the doorstep of Abba Aaron's house (par. 108): the dust of burial is the sure sign of resurrection. Another story makes it clear that such baptisms (whether through immersion or the sprinkling of water or earth) give new life: a childless woman hears about the stillborn baby brought to life and tells her husband to petition Abba Aaron for a male child. Aaron prays for the couple, and she bears a son (pars. 124–6).

All of these 'miracles' depend on the faith of the people who petition Abba Aaron. Their stories are like those in the Gospels where people call on Jesus: it is their great faith that allows them to be healed. But the faith—and power—of the holy man can bring a person to believe even when faith is lacking. One story, with more than a touch of humor to it, demonstrates this:

> Now it happened that one day two Nubians were walking together on their way to Aswan. One of them had only one eye. His friend said to him, 'Come on, let's receive a blessing at the hands of this great man'. The one-eyed man said, 'He isn't a great man; if he really is, let him open my eye', and while the words were still in his mouth, his eye—which had been blind—regained its sight, but his good eye became blind! When his friend saw what had happened, he was utterly amazed, and said to him, 'Didn't I tell you that he is a *very* great man?' The one-eyed man said, 'It's no great loss, for one eye has been shut while the other has been opened. However, let's go to him; perhaps he'll give light to the other eye'. So the two of them came to the

holy man Abba Aaron. My father said to the Nubian who was not a believer, 'Since you think that it's no great loss, why are you here?' Immediately he became very [fearful] and worshiped him, saying, '[Open my] eye!' and immediately he was able to see with the other eye. And the two believed, and went away joyful, and they proclaimed throughout that whole country the miracle that had taken place (par. 123).

This story reveals how Abba Aaron's power could work even at a distance. The miracle stories of this holy man, because of the sequence in which they are presented, show a progression in Aaron's power: the holy man first blesses water that heals; earth is then taken from in front of his house and sprinkled efficaciously on a stillborn child; a rich man is blinded because of Aaron's prayer and his sight is then restored by water blessed by the holy one; a gouty man believes he will be healed if the hand of someone healed by Aaron touches him and because of his faith, he is healed.

The powers of the holy man are very much like those of Jesus. Jesus healed by touching others; the woman with the hemorrhage was healed by touching Jesus' robe; the centurion's son was healed at a distance from Jesus because of his father's faith. Aaron himself affirms this similarity by quoting Jesus' words (Jn 14:12): 'Do not allow anyone to disbelieve our words. For indeed our Saviour said, "[Truly, truly, I say to you, whoever believes in me, the works which I do] he shall do also, for he shall do things greater than these"'.

Among the stories told about the early desert fathers Abba Aaron is not an isolated example. The monks took seriously the words of Jesus. Through belief in Christ one could heal the sick and raise the dead. What is striking, though, are the elements which the stories of Abba Aaron have in common with monastic stories from other parts of the Near East. Aphrahat (Aphraates), a syrian monk, was entreated by a 'pious man' to protect his land from a plague of locusts. He

> ordered a gallon of water to be brought to him. When the petitioner had brought the gallon, he placed his hand over it and besought God to fill the water with divine power; then on finishing the prayer he told the

man to sprinkle the water round the boundaries of his property. The man took it and did as instructed and it served as an invincible and inviolable defense for those fields. . . .[44]

The *Life of Pachomius* records that the holy man Theodore was so venerated that people 'would run forward, observe and take the soil on which the soles of his feet had stood and rub it on the sick'.[45]

John of Lycopolis 'did not perform cures publicly. More often he gave oil to the afflicted and healed them in that way'. A woman with cataracts begged to be taken to John, but he did not see women. She begged only that he should be told about her and offer a prayer for her. This he did, and moreover sent her some oil. She bathed her eyes in the oil only three times and on the third day regained her sight and publicly thanked God.[46] A woman suffering a long time with a flow of blood said to Abba Dionysius: 'I know that the man of God Abba Pachomius is your friend; therefore I want you to lead me to him so I may see him; for I am confident that if only I see him the Lord will grant me healing'. She went to see Pachomius, touched him and his clothing, and was healed.[47]

Holy men like Pachomius and Abba Aaron were intercessors. Because of their way of life, others believed that these holy men had immediate access to God; they were mediators with God. At times, holy men even seem to become substitutes for Christ—at least in the eyes of those who come to them for help. The writer of a letter to an Abba Paphnutius said to him, 'After God you are my salvation'. Popular belief often elevated holy men like Aaron to such a position. A man with a barren wife says to Aaron, '[I believe that] God will grant you [whatever you ask] from him', and the rich blind man says, 'Please ask Christ on my behalf that this darkness over my eyes cease, and I will never disobey *you* in anything'.[48]

---

[44] Theodoret of Cyrrhus, *A History of the Monks of Syria*, tr. by R.M. Price (Kalamazoo, 1985) 8.14; pp. 78–9.
[45] *Vita Pachomii* 150; Veilleux, p. 214.
[46] *Historia Monachorum* 1; Russell, p. 53.
[47] *Vita Pachomii* 41; Veilleux, pp. 64–5. For a series of miracles by Pachomius, see *Vita Pachomii* 41–5; Veilleux, pp. 64–9.
[48] Emphasis added.

Aaron resisted such exaltation. He always quotes the words of Jesus when speaking with those petitioning him. When a man has a son granted to him through the power of Aaron's prayer, he returns to Aaron with his son perched on his shoulder and exclaims, 'Look! The fruit which God has given to me through your holy intercessions!' Aaron takes the child in his arms and says, 'Blessed are *you*, Lord, in all *your* works'.[49]

The Way of Life

Abba Isaac, as a young man, sets out to find Abba Aaron because he has heard that Aaron lives 'the monastic life'. He goes out about three miles into the desert:

> After a while I looked down into the sand and I saw footprints headed around a corner in the rock. I followed them and found my holy father Abba Aaron, and hanging from his neck there was tied a large stone.
> Now when I called out to him, 'Bless me,' he withdrew his neck from the rope and threw the stone to the ground, and said to me, 'Where are you going, my son, in this place?' (Pars. 90–1).

Isaac, unlike the modern reader, shows absolutely no surprise at finding Aaron naked in the desert with a millstone tied around his neck. Aaron shows no distress at being found this way, and calmly gets dressed.

This brief story of Isaac's first encounter with Aaron is a miniature of the ascetical life of the anchorite. The aspirant journeys into the desert to search for a spiritual master. When he encounters him he finds that he is practising an ascetical discipline of the most severe kind. After he becomes a monk, Isaac must again journey into the desert in search of Abba Aaron:

> I discovered him standing out in the sand (it was very hot, since it was the season when the Nile floods). There was a huge stone sitting on his head and his eyeballs were about to burst on account of the heat.

---

[49]Emphasis added.

> He fell to the ground and gave himself up to die. I grabbed him and raised him up, weeping into his face, saying, 'Why do you punish yourself so badly like this, my holy father?' And he said to me, 'Why have you come here, my son' (par. 93)?

Isaac persists in his question, and Abba Aaron answers him:

> 'I will not hide anything from you, my son, regarding your question. Indeed,' he said, 'when I remember the afflictions which my good Saviour endured for us until he redeemed our race from the captivity of the Devil—he gave his body and blood for us—I say, "Since God took it upon himself to suffer on our behalf, it is right that we too should have every kind of affliction until he has mercy on us on the day of reckoning."' And when he had said these things, we rose that day and left and came home (par. 94).

Aaron's answer is deeply—uncomfortably—incarnational and reflects a profound *imitatio Christi*: to imitate Christ is a eucharistic sacrifice. The technical terms *ascesis* (ascetical practice) and *apatheia* (the denial of the passions which deflect one from God) rarely occur in the two pieces attributed to Paphnutius and are not treated in a systematic way.[50] Detailed descriptions of monastic ascetical practice are not given. Offered, instead, are stories about a way of life. 'The Life of Abba Aaron' (part three of the *Histories of the Monks of Upper Egypt*) and the *Life of Onnophrius* are the story of a monk—in this case, Paphnutius—traveling into the desert to inquire about the way of life of the holy ones. Within that frame are many smaller frames, individual stories, of other monks making a similar journey and seeking the same truth.

Abba Aaron, perhaps wearied by spiritual tourists and thrill-seekers, tells Isaac early in the latter's 'novitiate': 'The monastic life has become well-known, but this way of life is work and suffering up to the very end'.[51] What is this life of which

---

[50] For a discussion of these terms, see Russell, p. 125, n.17 and p. 126, n.22, who refers the reader to more detailed sources.

[51] Par. 91. Palamon, to whom Pachomius attaches himself, warns Pachomius, 'This work of God is not so simple; for many have come but have not persevered' (G 1, par. 6; Veilleux, p. 301).

Aaron speaks? It is a life of *hesychia*, 'of quiet contemplation glorifying God' (par. 91).[52] Timothy tells Paphnutius that one day while he was living in a community of monks, 'there came into my heart a thought of this kind: "Rise and go, and stay in a place by yourself. You will lead a life of quiet contemplation [*hesychia*] as an anchorite"' (*Onnophrius*, par. 5). Timothy goes on to define 'quiet contemplation': (1) 'You will welcome the brethren'. (2) 'You will show great hospitality to the stranger', (3) 'and you will earn more than enough through the work of your hands'.

Two very important points are made here: the first concern is not for the self, but for others; there is no mention of prayer. At the root of monastic spirituality lies hospitality, not just in the sense of *receiving* others, but also in the sense of *reaching out* to others. This is *hesychia*, and joined with it is prayer and the quiet handiwork of a contemplative life. Young Pachomius is seized by the 'Spirit of God', and the Spirit tells him, 'Struggle and settle down here': 'The thing pleased him and he settled down there, growing some vegetables and some palm-trees in order to feed himself or some poor man in the village or again some stranger who should happen to pass by in a boat or on the road'.[53]

A life of prayer is essential to the monk if he or she is to maintain a life of quiet contemplation. Prayer, in fact, is inseparable from *hesychia*. Onnophrius tells Paphnutius, 'We lived together a life of quiet contemplation, glorifying God. Now I would spend the night in vigil with them and I learned the rules of God from them' (*Onnophrius*, par. 7). The 'rules of God' involved spiritual discipline and fasting (ascesis), manual work, prayer, and the recitation of Scripture. Palamon said to Pachomius:

> The rule of monastic life, according to what we have learned from those who went before us, is as follows: We always spend half the night, and often even from

---

[52] Russell, p. 49, translates *hesychia* as 'stillness'. He notes, p. 123 n.8, that *hesychia* is 'already a technical term expressing the state of inner tranquility and silence which follows the victory over the passions'. Louis Bouyer, *Cosmos* (Petersham, Mass. 1988), p. 53, notes that '...the essential virtues of a wise man, in Egyptian eyes, were attentive silence and patience'.

[53] *Vita Pachomii* 8; Veilleux, p. 28.

> evening to morning, in vigils and the recitation of the words of God, also doing manual work with threads, hairs, or palm-fibers, lest we be overcome by sleep. [We do this work] for our bodily subsistence also; and whatever is above and beyond our needs we give to the poor, following the words of the Apostle, 'only let us remember the poor' (Gal 2:10).[54]

When the monk perseveres in *ascesis* and *hesychia*, Onnophrius tells Paphnutius, God sends the holy angels to give charge over him and the trees of the earth produce fruit year around, enough for his needs (par. 16). The monk is like the lilies of the fields and the birds of the air.

The monastic journey of *hesychia* was best made, according to the early egyptian monks, with a spiritual advisor or holy man. Isaac finds Aaron; Pachomius, after three years in Seneset, seeks out 'an ancient ascetic', Abba Palamon, 'a holy old man'. When Pachomius knocks on the door of Palamon's cell, the old man—like Abba Aaron—tells him that the journey will not be an easy one.[55] Pachomius stays with Palamon, as Isaac does with Aaron:

> After the old man had tried him for three full months and had seen his courage and his firm determination, he took a monk's habit with the belt and he placed it before the altar, and they spent the whole night praying over them. Then he clothed him with it at daybreak and they celebrated the morning prayer together with joy.[56]

Aaron does not himself accept Isaac into monastic life, but takes him to a priest:

> he took me to a priest to clothe me in the monastic habit. And when we called inside the priest's house he came outside and greeted us and took us inside his place. Right away my father told him about me and

---

[54] *Vita Pachomii* 10; p. 31. See also 15; p. 38.
[55] *Vita Pachomii* 10; pp. 29–30.
[56] *Vita Pachomii* 10; p. 32.

immediately the priest shaved the hair from my head and clothed me in the monastic habit. We rose and went home. Now my holy father Aaron spent a week in helping me lay the foundations for doing good work in the service of God.[57]

Obedience in the paphnutian literature, as in the *Apophthegmata*, is obedience to a spiritual master, freely chosen. In cenobitic monasticism, this became obedience 'to a superior officially recognized as the head of a community and, at the same time, obedience to a whole collection of codified regulations'.[58] The monasticism described by Paphnutius is mostly that of anchorites and small groups of men not attached to large communities. And yet, the key elements of cenobitic monasticism—the master, the rule, and the community—are vitally in evidence.

The master, the rule, and the community stabilized the life of the anchorites. Although stability was crucial to the monk as a safeguard against extreme idiosyncrasy and individualism, the theme of the journey persists alongside of it: '. . . the primitive feeling, so strongly expressed in the *Vita Antonii*, would persist: that the monk is someone who can never halt, never settle down anywhere. This is the theme of journeying as did Abraham, the theme which Origen, after Philo, had developed so forcefully'.[59] Journeying lies at the heart of the stories told by Paphnutius, the story of Abba Pambo, and the stories in the *Historia Monachorum*. And despite all the seeming differences between the monastic journey and the journey of the ordinary Christian, they share the same goal: the finding of a spiritual home, coming to a deeper knowledge of God.

When Isaac finds Abba Aaron in the formidable desert, Aaron asks him, 'Where are you going, my son?' Isaac responds, 'Forgive me, my father, for I am lost.' 'Come, sit down, my son,' Aaron replies simply. 'Indeed, you are not lost; rather, you have found the good path'.

---

[57]Par.92. Benedicta Ward, in Russell, p. 25, gives a description of the monastic habit. Copres 'describes a short-sleeved tunic, a hood, a sheepskin cloak, a linen cloth around the waist'. The clothing was placed upon a disciple by his spiritual master.
[58]Bouyer, *History*, p. 325.
[59]Bouyer, *History*, p. 326.

PAPHNUTIUS

In the fourth and fifth centuries the name Paphnutius—in Coptic, Papnoute, the one belonging to God—may have been the Smith or Jones of coptic-speaking Egypt.[60] When unsuspecting readers try to sort out the various Paphnutiuses known to history, they first feel like a person who is handed the phone book of any large american city and is told simply to find Mr Smith. The effort is worthwhile, however, because it is possible to be reasonably certain about the Paphnutius who wrote the *Histories of the Monks of Upper Egypt* and the *Life of Onnophrius*.

Before we attempt to discover which of the Paphnutiuses known to history wrote the *Histories of the Monks of Upper Egypt* and the *Life of Onnophrius*, we must first make a list of the most important of the men known by this name, with a brief description of each.[61]

(1) The most famous Paphnutius is the confessor and bishop, a 'martyr without bloodshed', whose feast day is celebrated on 11 September (Coptic 9 February and 1 May).[62] Tradition has it that this Paphnutius, a bishop in the Thebaid, died around 360. He has been seen as a disciple of Anthony and a supporter of Athanasius. 'He suffered such hardship and cruelty during the persecution by Maximin Daza (305–313) that at the Council of Nicea his

---

[60] Armand Veilleux comments that 'one must not forget that Paphnoute and Pachomius were among the most common Coptic names. The *Life of Pachomius* mentions two Pachomiuses and at least two Paphnoutes if not three.' Veilleux, 'Monasticism and Gnosis in Egypt', in Birger A. Pearson and James E. Goehring, eds., *The Roots of Egyptian Christianity* (Philadelphia, 1986) p. 281. A Paphnutius was the brother of Theodore, the disciple of Pachomius, and for many years the great steward of the *koinonia* at Phbow. See Veilleux, ed., *Pachomian Koinonia*, 1:291 (par. 181, n.1). 'Papnoute' occurs as a grafitto on a limestone cliff near Thebes. See Winlock and Crum, *The Monastery of Epiphanius at Thebes* 1:7. On the various spellings of Paphnoute in the papyri, see H.I. Bell, *Jews and Christians in Egypt* (London, 1924) p. 100. I have decided to use in this volume the traditional, latinized, versions of coptic names.

[61] The list here is not exhaustive. For other lists, see De Lacy O'Leary, *The Saints of Egypt* (London and New York, 1937) 219–221; H. Leclercq, 'Paphnuce', *Dictionnaire d'archéologie chrétienne et de liturgie*, 13/1:1358–61, who lists those known from the papyri; Dom Cuthbert Butler, ed., *The Lausiac History of Palladius* (London, 1898) 2:224–5, n. 89; Bell, pp. 100–104.

[62] Friedhelm Winkelmann, 'Paphnutios, der Bekenner und Bischof', in Peter Nagel, ed., *Probleme der koptischen Literatur* (Halle, 1968) 145. See also O'Leary, 218. The epithet is from O'Leary.

mutilated body was an object of wonder and veneration to the assembled bishops'.⁶³

(2) Epiphanius, bishop of Salamis and indefatigable cataloguer of heresies, numbers a certain Paphnutius in a list of melitian schismatics.⁶⁴ The son of a confessor, this Paphnutius was a confessor and anchorite, and not a bishop.

It is difficult to distinguish between these two Paphnutiuses, and it is possible that the melitian Paphnutius and the famous confessor and supporter of Athanasius were, in fact, confused in antiquity and were one and the same person.⁶⁵ The fourth-century sources do not know of a confessor Paphnutius who was a bishop.⁶⁶ Furthermore, the nicean stories are legendary, the sources are not clear that Paphnutius died in 360, and it is difficult to prove that he became a monk in 311.⁶⁷

Whether or not one believes that the two confessors—orthodox and melitian—are one, the uncertainty clearly shows how difficult the terrain is for anyone gathering evidence about egyptian Christianity in the fourth and fifth centuries; this will serve as a cautionary reminder to us as we seek to discover the author of the *Histories of the Monks of Upper Egypt* and the *Life of Onnophrius*.⁶⁸

(3) Paphnutius the martyr died with 546 other Christians during the persecution of Diocletian.⁶⁹

---

⁶³Cross and Livingstone, eds., *The Oxford Dictionary of the Christian Church* 1028. This is the only Paphnutius the *Dictionary* lists.

⁶⁴Epiphanius, *Panarion* 68.5.3.

⁶⁵This is Winkelmann's hypothesis; see pp. 145–153.

⁶⁶Winkelmann, 151.

⁶⁷Winkelmann, 152.

⁶⁸Winkelmann's conclusions run thus: Gelasius at the end of the fourth century is the first to name the orthodox confessor Paphnutius. He is a θεοῦ ἄνθρωπος, a person of God, and a confessor, but he is not called an anchorite or bishop (p. 146). Gelasius' *Vorlage*, he concludes, did not know of Paphnutius the bishop (p. 147). Paphnutius is named bishop in a suspect latin translation of Rufinus, and it is very questionable whether he is listed as one of the bishops subscribing to Nicea (pp. 147–8). Epiphanius is more trustworthy here than Gelasius or Rufinus (149), and the Paphnutius who is the follower of Anthony is not to be equated with the famous confessor (p. 151). The irony is, he concludes, that what evidence we do have fits best if Paphnutius 'the Great', the orthodox hero, is identical to the melitian schismatic identified by Epiphanius (p. 152).

⁶⁹Martyred by Arianus, this Paphnutius died on 20 Pharmuthi (15 April). See O'Leary, p. 217. The *Oxford Dictionary of the Christian Church*, p. 1028, incorrectly attributes the greek *Passio* of this Paphnutius to the confessor who died in 360 (#1). For the coptic text of the *Martyrdom of Paphnutius*, see I. Balestri

(4) Palladius, in the *Lausiac History* 46, mentions a certain Paphnutius who was one of a number of monks and bishops banished to Diocaesarea in 374. It is probable that these monks and bishops were banished as part of the arian persecution which took place after the death of Athanasius and the intrusion of Lucius into the see of Alexandria.[70] This Paphnutius, called 'Paphnutius of Scetis', was living in Nitria when Melania the Elder, friend of Rufinus and founder of a monastery on the Mount of Olives, met him on her journeys through Egypt.

(5) Palladius (*Lausiac History* 18) mentions another Paphnutius who was a disciple of Macarius of Alexandria, but the *Apophthegmata* (the sayings of the desert fathers) make him a disciple of Macarius of Egypt.[71] Since the two Macariuses are often confused in the monastic sources, it is not surprising that their disciples are also. The coptic sources say that this Paphnutius succeeded Macarius as presbyter in Scetis; Cassian, however, reports that Paphnutius succeeded Isidore (see below, p. 47).[72]

(6) Paphnutius appears with the two Macariuses and Serapion as the author of a Regula Patrum in the *Codex Regularum*.[73]

(7) A collection of papyri letters addressed to a certain Paphnutius can be dated to the middle of the fourth century. It offers a fascinating glimpse of the role holy men played in late antiquity (see above, pp. 30–37).[74] Many of these letters are petitions to Paphnutius asking for help or intercession. Many people 'resorted to the holy man in person; those who could not do that appealed to him by letters. . . .'[75]

One letter in particular forcefully illustrates the high esteem in which the monk as holy man was held:

---

and H. Hyvernat, eds., *Acta Martyrum* I (textus) pp. 110–19, and the latin translation in I (versio) pp. 72–77. For the greek text, see H. Delehaye, 'Les martyrs d'Égypte', *Analecta Bollandiana* 40 (1922) 328–343.

[70]Butler, 2:223, n.86. See also O'Leary, pp. 220–1.

[71]See Macarius of Egypt, #28 and #37; Benedicta Ward, tr., *The Sayings of the Desert Fathers* (Kalamazoo, 1984) 133 and 136.

[72]Butler, 2:224. n.89. On Paphnutius the successor of Macarius at Scetis, see Hugh G. Evelyn White, *The Monasteries of the Wâdi 'N Natrûn*, Part II, *The History of the Monasteries of Nitria and Scetis* (New York: The Metropolitan Museum of Art, 1932 [repr. 1973]) 120–122.

[73]Butler, 2:224, n.89.

[74]Bell, p. 100.

[75]Bell, p. 103.

To the beloved and most pious and dear to God and blessed father Paphnuthius, Ammonius greetings in the Lord God. I always know that by your holy prayers I shall be saved from every temptation of the Devil and from every contrivance of men, and now I beg you to remember me in your holy prayers; for after God you are my salvation. Our brother Didymus came to see me, and I met him according to your instructions in the matter. I pray for your health for many years, most sweet father; may the God of peace preserve you for a great length of time.[76]

The Paphnutius who received this letter (and the others in the collection) was probably an orthodox anchorite, and may have been Paphnutius Cephalas (see below, p. 46).[77]

(8) The *Historia Monachorum in Aegypto* devotes a chapter to a monk named Paphnutius. Travellers visiting monastic sites describe Paphnutius as an anchorite who lived in the vicinity of Heracleopolis in the Fayum (the Thebaid). He was 'a great and virtuous man who had died not long before'.[78] The journey of the author or authors of the *Historia Monachorum* is usually dated 394–5, which would mean that this Paphnutius died probably sometime between 390 and 394.[79]

The story the *Historia Monachorum* tells about Paphnutius is delightful. 'After many years of *ascesis*', Paphnutius 'asked God to make known to him which of the saints who had lived a virtuous life he most resembled'.[80] An angel of the Lord surprises him by likening him not to a venerated saint or ascetic but to three worldlings: a flute player, the head of a neighboring village, and finally a merchant seeking fine pearls.[81] Paphnutius visits each in turn and each relates to him his way of life. Each is virtuous

---

[76]Bell, p. 104.

[77]Bell's conclusion, p. 102.

[78]Russell, tr., p. 95. The syriac version of the *Historia Monachorum* confirms this detail. See E.A. Wallis Budge, *The Paradise or Garden of the Fathers...* (London, 1907) 1:358–62.

[79]See Benedicta Ward's introduction in Russell, pp. 4–5; and Owen Chadwick, *John Cassian* (London, 1968) p. 7.

[80]Russell, p. 95.

[81]For 'worldlings', as opposed to 'monks' (which is what this Paphnutius expected), Helmut Brunner uses the apt word 'Weltmann'. See Brunner, 'Eine

(the village leader recites a litany of hospitality worthy of Job), but Paphnutius tells each that he is not perfect: to be perfect he must become a monk, so each one drops everything and follows him.[82] Each then lives a truly virtuous life, is perfected, and goes to heaven. Finally, Paphnutius is summoned to heaven by a choir of prophets.[83]

It is likely that the Paphnutius of the *Historia Monachorum* is not identical with the Paphnutius Cephalas or the Paphnutius Bubalis mentioned respectively by Palladius and Cassian, descriptions of whom now follow.[84] These two are the most likely candidates for the authorship of the *Histories of the Monks of Upper Egypt* and the *Life of Onnophrius*.

(9) Palladius, in the *Lausiac History*, reports meeting a certain Paphnutius Cephalas.[85] 'He had the gift of divine knowledge of Sacred Scripture, both the Old and the New Testament, explaining them without ever having read the writings, but he was so meek that his prophetic gift was hidden. Of him it is reported that in eighty years he never wore two tunics at once'.[86]

Palladius traveled around Egypt in the 390s, and if this Paphnutius Cephalas was indeed a very old man of eighty or more, then he would have been a living witness to the dawn of monasticism at the beginning of the fourth century.[87] The *Apophthegmata* do indeed connect Paphnutius Cephalas with Saint Anthony. In one saying, Paphnutius, 'who is called Cephalas', is with Anthony and is praised by the great old man as one 'who can care for souls and save them'.[88]

The sayings of the fathers also locate Paphnutius in Scetis (or

---

altägyptische Idealbiographie in christlichen Gewande', *Zeitschrift für Ägyptische Sprache und Altertumskunde* 99.Ib (1973) 90.

[82]For a detailed discussion of this text, especially with regard to Rufinus' translation, see Brunner, 90–94. Brunner suggests that paragraph 13, the headmaster's litany, stands in close relationship to ancient Egyptian *Idealbiographie*, and gives a detailed discussion, 91–94. But it seems to me that the book of Job also lies in the background (see Job 29:11–20).

[83]Russell, pp. 95–98.

[84]Butler's conclusion, 2:224, n.89.

[85]Παφνουτίου τοῦ ἐπιλεγομένου Κεφαλᾶ. See Lausiac History 47 (Butler ed., 2:137). His feast day is 15 Amshir (9 February); see O'Leary, p. 219.

[86]*Lausiac History* 47.3; Meyer, p. 125.

[87]On Palladius' chronology, see Meyer, p. 5; Butler, pp. 179–80. Chitty, p. 210, dates his visit to Nitria and the Cells to 390-2.

[88]The alphabetical collection, #29 (under Anthony); Ward, p. 7.

Scete), the collection of monasteries in the desert immediately south of Alexandria (the Wadi Natrun). In one saying, Paphnutius is described as the 'Father of Scetis', and seems to have been a person of authority there. Whether he was lay or ordained is unclear. Abba Eudemon said: 'I went down there while I was still young and he would not let me stay, saying to me, "I do not allow the face of a woman to dwell in Scetis, because of the conflict with the enemy" '.[89] One thing is very striking: none of the sayings attributed to Paphnutius—and which locate him in Scetis—gives him the nickname Cephalas.[90]

(10) Corroboration for a monk named Paphnutius who lived at Scetis comes from Cassian, who visited that desert community sometime between 385 and 399.[91] This Paphnutius, however, is a priest—and his nickname is 'Bubalus' or 'Bubalis', the 'wild ox' or 'buffalo'! As Cassian reports:

> He is now the priest in that desert of Scete which is renowned and which ought to be famous everywhere. Now Paphnutius has displayed such a love of the hidden life that the other anchorites have nicknamed him Bubalus. They have called him the Wild Ox because of this innate longing he has for solitude, because of the joy he has in always being alone.[92]

According to Cassian, Paphnutius succeeded Isidore 'as priest in the desert', but he must have ministered to his 'parish' from his cell—or from a long spiritual distance.[93] This 'priest for that group of ours which was in the desert...even as a very old man...never moved from the cell occupied by him since the

---

[89]Ward, p. 64.

[90]Also observed by Butler, 2:224, n.89. In the syriac translation of the *Apophthegmata*, Paphnutius is identified as a disciple of Macarius (three times), a contemporary of Anthony (once), as Paphnutius 'the Simple, who was from Scetis' (once), and is unidentified in the remaining sayings. See E.A. Wallis Budge, *The Wit and Wisdom of the Desert* (Oxford, 1934), index, p. 445.

[91]Chadwick, p. 15.

[92]Cassian, *Conferences* 18.5; John Cassian, *Conferences*, tr. Colm Luibheid (New York, 1985) p. 196.

[93]Cassian 18.5; Luibheid, p. 196. O'Leary, p. 219, says that around 373 Paphnutius succeeded Isidore as priest of 'the primary community of Scetis', and after the death of Saint Macarius shortly before 390 became 'father of Scetis'. Isidore was banished in 374 with, apparently, a different Paphnutius. See above, note 70.

time when he was quite young and which was five miles from the church'.⁹⁴

But such isolation was not enough for Paphnutius because 'he had a feverish urge to move ever higher and hurried forward to enter into the secrets of the desert. Living amid the throng of his brethren he thirsted to get away from the distraction of human company and to be totally at one with the Lord':

> Racked by his longing for unceasing contemplation of God, he kept away from the sight of all, pushed farther and farther into the remote and inaccessible regions of the desert and hid there for a long time. Indeed he was rarely—and only with difficulty—found by the anchorites themselves. There was a belief that he enjoyed each day the delight of meeting with the angels. And because of this longing of his to be away from everyone he was given the nickname Bubalis. . . .⁹⁵

According to Cassian, Paphnutius Bubalis was over ninety at the end of the fourth century.⁹⁶ In 399, Theophilus, bishop of Alexandria, issued an Easter letter in which he attacked anthropomorphism, the 'heresy' (according to Cassian) which understood God in terms too human. It was a letter 'received very bitterly by almost every sort of monk throughout all Egypt'.⁹⁷ The monks of Scetis denounced Theophilus' letter. 'Among all the priests only our own Paphnutius was an exception. Those in charge of the three other churches in the desert [of Scetis] refused to allow the letter to be read or publicly presented at their assemblies'.⁹⁸

Are Paphnutius Cephalas and Paphnutius Bubalis one and the same person?⁹⁹ It certainly seems possible. Both Palladius and

---

⁹⁴Cassian, 3.1; Luibheid p. 81.
⁹⁵Ibid., pp. 81–82.
⁹⁶Ibid., p. 81.
⁹⁷Cassian, 10.2; Luibheid, pp. 125–6.
⁹⁸Ibid. On anthropomorphism, see *Conferences* 10.2. The anthropomorphites believed that God the Father was of a human shape. They believed that they were supported by scripture in this and that there was 'clear scriptural evidence' that Adam was created in God's very image.
⁹⁹Owen Chadwick suggests that the two are one person. See *John Cassian*, p. 15, n.1. Chadwick identifies both Paphnutiuses as followers of Origen. Caution is warranted here. Cassian's Paphnutius (*Conferences* 10.2–3) was certainly opposed to anthropomorphism, but that does not automatically make him an Origenist.

Cassian place a Paphnutius at Scetis in the last decade of the fourth century, and both describe him as a venerated old man. There are, however, important differences: they have different nicknames (names not readily confused!), and Cassian's Paphnutius is a priest and leader of Scetis.

Dom Cuthbert Butler, in his great edition of the *Lausiac History*, pointed out that the doctrine attributed to Paphnutius Cephalas by Palladius (*Lausiac History* 47) ought to be compared with that attributed to Paphnutius Bubalis by Cassian (*Conferences* 3). Butler concluded that 'it is difficult to escape from the conclusion that Cassian here borrowed his thought from Palladius'.[100] If one accepts Butler's conclusion (and it is a reasonable one), then one has to wonder about the separate identity of the two Paphnutiuses. Who was the Paphnutius whom Cassian visited? And, one would like to inquire further of Cassian, what was his nickname?

Butler, moreover, implicitly pointed to a further difficulty. If the words of Cassian's Paphnutius are borrowed from the Paphnutius of Palladius, to whom should we attribute these words? Palladius himself? Most likely. By no means is this to suggest that Palladius and Cassian have created the figure(s) of Paphnutius *ex nihilo*.[101] It is a commonplace that ancient historians, from Thucydides onwards, were not concerned about being stenographers to those whose speech they recorded. Because the words attributed to Saint Paul in his speech on the Areopagus are more likely to belong to Luke than to Paul does not mean that Paul did not speak there at all.

The evidence *does* argue overwhelmingly for one or two monks named Paphnutius who were held in high esteem at the end of the fourth century. Despite the uncertainties that Palladius and Cassian present, the earliest sources—the sayings of the fathers, the oral traditions handed on to Palladius and Cassian, and the two writers themselves as eyewitnesses—place a Paphnutius, an old man and venerated monk, at Scetis at the end of the fourth

---

From *Lausiac History* 47, it is not clear, at least to me, that this Paphnutius is an Origenist. Tillemont believed that all the Paphnutiuses were one; see Butler, 2:224, n.89.

[100] Ibid.

[101] For Palladius as a historian, see Butler, 1:203–8; for Cassian, see Chadwick, pp. 18–30.

century. This Paphnutius, probably Paphnutius 'Cephalas', is the most likely author of the *Histories of the Monks of Upper Egypt* and the *Life of Onnophrius*.

THE HISTORIES OF THE MONKS OF UPPER EGYPT

The title *Histories of the Monks of Upper Egypt* is the present author's. In 1914–15, E.A. Wallis Budge published his important collection *Coptic Texts* from manuscripts in the oriental collection of the British Museum.[102] In volume IV, Budge edited and translated 'The Life of Apa Onnophrios the Anchorite' by Paphnutius, and in volume V '[Histories of the Monks in the Egyptian Desert by Paphnutius]'.[103] The manuscript of the *Histories* is damaged and the beginning is missing, which includes the title page.[104] Budge therefore gave the manuscript a title, and his title has been generally accepted by more recent commentators.[105]

For the present volume I have emended the title to *Histories of the Monks of Upper Egypt* to make it more specific and indicate more accurately the contents of the narrative. The narrative by Paphnutius falls into three parts:[106] (1) Paphnutius meets with a monk named Pseleusius and other monastic brethren at an unnamed location, but it is clear that they are in the Thebaid in Upper Egypt and, more specifically, in the vicinity of Aswan and Philae: Arianus and Paul, two monks, come from Aswan (paragraph 12), and Isaac, another monk, lives 'on an island in the

---

[102] These are now in the British Library. See Bentley Layton, *Catalogue of Coptic Literary Manuscripts in the British Library* (London, 1987).

[103] 'The Life of Onnophrios' by Paphnutius is found in E.A. Wallis Budge, *Coptic Texts*, IV, *Coptic Martyrdoms, Etc. in the Dialect of Upper Egypt* (London, 1914 [repr. New York, 1977]). Budge's summary is on pp. lxiv–lxviii; the coptic text occupies pp. 205–224 and the english translation pp. 455–73. The '[Histories of the Monks in the Egyptian Desert by Paphnutius]' is found in Budge, *Coptic Texts*, V: *Miscellaneous Coptic Texts* (London, 1915 [repr. New York, 1977]). Budge's summary is in volume V, pt. 1, pp. cxliv–clvi; the coptic text occupies V/1, pp. 432–95 (with scripture readings appointed for the feast day of Abba Aaron appended, pp. 496–502), and the english translation in V/2:948–1011.

[104] Budge (V/1:lvi) suggests that 'one or two leaves' are missing. Layton, p. 196, says one leaf.

[105] O'Leary, p. 220, uses the title 'Stories of the Monks of the Desert', and he has been followed in this by Layton, p. 196.

[106] As Layton, p. 197, has observed.

middle of the [first] cataract', four miles south of the community where Paphnutius first meets the brethren (par. 26). Philae was at the first cataract and Aswan, according to the twelfth-century traveler Abû Ṣâliḥ, was five miles north of Philae. (2) Isaac tells Paphnutius the history of the bishops of Philae (pars. 29–85). (3) Isaac narrates the life of Abba Aaron, a monk who lived near Aswan (pars. 86–138).

Since a large portion of the *Histories* is devoted to the life and works of Abba Aaron, and since the narrative ends with his story and appends lectionary readings for his feast day, it is possible that the original title of this work was *The Life of Abba Aaron*.[107] But since that is uncertain, and since all the action of the narrative occurs in upper Egypt in the vicinity of Aswan and Philae, I have chosen the present title.

By 'Histories' I intend to suggest both 'story', as in a narrative, and 'history': this was the sense *historia* had in both later classical and patristic Greek.[108] The section of the *Histories of the Monks of Upper Egypt* devoted to Abba Aaron is a collection of stories as remembered and lovingly told by a disciple: we are witnesses to oral tradition becoming, in a sense, canonized. The story of the first bishops of Philae is also a collection of stories already made legendary, but it is also an attempt to provide a history of the Church at Philae from its beginnings; this narrative may, in fact, be based on local 'historical' records (see below, 'Aswan and Philae: The Origins of Christianity in Upper Egypt', pp. 54–69).

Scholarly tradition has attributed the *Histories of the Monks of Upper Egypt* to Paphnutius Cephalas (see above, pp. 42–50).[109]

---

[107]For an analogous example, see the 'Life of Abba Cyrus' in Budge, *Coptic Martyrdoms*, pp. 128–136 and 381–89. Cyrus is the last (and, to the story, the most important) monk visited by an Abba Pambo. The story is really about Pambo and his spiritual journey. See Vivian, 'Journeying into God'. The *Life of Onnophrius* in the present volume follows a similar pattern: only part of the narrative is concerned with Onnophrius.

[108]See Liddell and Scott, 842A, and Lampe, 678B.

[109]There is, interestingly, no ancient attribution (outside of the manuscripts) of these texts to any Paphnutius. Budge, *Miscellaneous Coptic Texts* pt. 1, pp. cxliv–cxlv, says that it 'probably' belongs to Paphnutius Cephalas, the author of the *Life of Onnophrius*. O'Leary, pp. 219–20, attributes both the *Histories* and the *Life* to Paphnutius Cephalas. Layton, pp. 172, 192, and 196, also attributes both texts to 'Paphnutius Cephalas (the Hermit)'.

There is, however, no evidence in the manuscripts for attributing the authorship to a specific Paphnutius. The name 'Paphnutius' occurs five times in the *Histories* (pars 26–28, 88, and 137), and Paphnutius is clearly the person to whom the stories and history of the monks of upper Egypt are being told. But this Paphnutius is never given a nickname; nor are we told where he comes from. At the end of the narrative we learn that he is about to set out on a journey north (and, one presumes, home). The title page of the manuscript may have contained more specific information about Paphnutius; its loss is decisive here.

The *Life of Onnophrius* begins by saying that the story is narrated by 'a certain brother, an anchorite by the name of Abba Paphnutius' (par. 1), and the Coda clearly places him in Scetis (par. 37), where several Paphnutiuses were reported to have lived, including Paphnutius Cephalas and Paphnutius Bubalis (see above, pp. 46–48). Neither the *Histories* nor the *Life of Onnophrius* identifies Paphnutius more precisely.

More positively, it is possible to date fairly precisely the 'action' reported in the *Histories of the Monks of Upper Egypt*. According to the narrative, the first bishop of Philae was Macedonius; he was consecrated by Athanasius, bishop of Alexandria from 328–373.[110] Macedonius' successor, Mark, also went to Alexandria to be consecrated by Athanasius, and it is just possible that he is mentioned in a letter of Athanasius from the year 362 (see below, p. 65–66).[111] Mark was succeeded by Isaiah. His successor, Pseleusias (not to be confused with the monk Pseleusius at the beginning of the *Histories*), is also consecrated in Alexandria; the bishop is not named, but was most likely Timothy, bishop from 381–85.[112] Pseleusias later returns north for the consecration of Theophilus as bishop of Alexandria: 'all the bishops went to Alexandria to pay their respects to him'.[113] Theophilus' accession to the see of Alexandria can be firmly dated to 385. He is the last bishop of Alexandria named in the text.

Pseleusias is the last bishop of Philae to be mentioned, but the sequence of events is not clear in the narrative. When Abba

---

[110] Par. 30.
[111] Pars. 56–61.
[112] Pars. 80–83.
[113] Par. 83.

Aaron dies he is buried beside the three bishops of Philae—Macedonius, Mark, and Isaiah—which must indicate that Pseleusias is still living and is bishop of Philae at the time of Aaron's death.[114] Yet the death of Pseleusias is recounted earlier.[115] To add to the confusion, Aaron is referred to at one point as a bishop but nothing in the lengthy narrative devoted to his life substantiates this. The successor of Pseleusias is not known, nor is his date of succession, so it is not possible to supply a closing date for the narrative. If the frame of the narrative is historical—that is, Paphnutius' visit to upper Egypt and his being told the history of the bishops of Philae (the more legendary aspects of the history do not deny its basic credibility)—and I believe it is, then it seems reasonable to suggest that Paphnutius visited the region of Aswan and Philae sometime after 385. A date of 390–400 seems reasonable.

How does such a date fit with the Paphnutiuses known to us? The Paphnutius of the *Historia Monachorum* (see above, pp. 45–46) died sometime in the early 390s, so it is possible that he is the author. He lived apparently near Heracleopolis in the Fayum and could easily have made a journey upriver to Aswan and Philae.

Both Palladius and Cassian, as we have seen, place a Paphnutius in Scetis in the 390s. The *Life of Onnophrius* also locates Paphnutius in Scetis. It is possible, however, that the author of the *Life* is different from the author of the *Histories*. We have three candidates who can reasonably be supposed to have written the *Histories of the Monks of Upper Egypt*: Paphnutius of Heracleopolis, Paphnutius Bubalis, and Paphnutius Cephalas. It is difficult to reconcile the solitary character of Paphnutius Bubalis, as described by Cassian, with the gregariousness of the Paphnutius who travels through the pages of the *Histories* and the *Life of Onnophrius*. Paphnutius Cephalas remains the most likely author of the *Histories*. Around 390 he would have been a very old man, but advanced age does not rule him out as the author; Saint Anthony lived to a very old age, as, it seems, did many of the monks in Egypt.

One thing is certain: a Paphnutius, probably to be identified with Paphnutius Cephalas, *did* make such a journey and *did* listen to the stories of monks living in the area of Aswan and Philae.

---

[114]Par. 138.
[115]Par. 85.

These monks, as the story of Abba Aaron and the history of the bishops of Philae make clear, were themselves conservers of a tradition, the tradition of monastic Christianity at Philae. In the persons of Abba Aaron and Bishop Macedonius, their history in upper Egypt appears to go back to the middle of the fourth century. If this is so, then what they have to say is very important, not only for our understanding of monastic practices and customs in the fourth century, but also for our knowledge of the origins of Christianity at Aswan and Philae at the outer edge of the Roman Empire.

ASWAN AND PHILAE: THE ORIGINS OF CHRISTIANITY IN UPPER EGYPT[116]

Aswan and Philae, although famous in ancient egyptian history, are relatively unknown during the coptic and christian era. Aswan was famous in pharaonic times for its great monuments, and Philae was equally well known during ptolemaic and roman times for its temple of Isis.[117]

Historians of christian monasticism in Egypt have paid little attention to Aswan and Philae and their neglect is charted, as it were, on the maps that accompany their studies. Benedicta Ward's translation of the *Apophthegmata patrum* contains a map entitled

---

[116]For general studies on Egypt and early egyptian Christianity, see Alan K. Bowman, *Egypt After the Pharoahs* (London, 1986) and C. Wilfred Griggs, *Early Egyptian Christianity from its Origins to 451 C.E.* (Coptic Studies 2; Leiden, 1990). For a good recent overview of Egypt, Christianity, and early monasticism, see Samuel Rubenson, *The Letters of Saint Antony: Origenist Theology, Monastic Tradition and the Making of a Saint* (Lund, 1990) 89–125. On the origins of monasticism in Egypt, see Hans Lietzmann's sometimes unsympathetic assessment in *The Era of the Church Fathers*, volume 4 of *A History of the Early Church* (New York, 1952) 124–202. See also Karl Heussi, *Der Ursprung des Mönchtums in der alten Kirche* (Tübingen, 1936), Bernhard Lohse, *Askese und Mönchtum in der Antike und in der alten Kirche* (Munich/Vienna, 1969), and James E. Goehring, 'The Origins of Monasticism', in *Eusebius, Judaism, and Christianity* (Detroit: Wayne State, 1992).

[117]H. Leclercq, 'Philae', *Dictionnaire d'archéologie chrétienne et de liturgie*, 13/1:692. For a brief history of pharaonic Philae, see William Y. Adams, *Nubia: Corridor to Africa* (Princeton, 1977) p. 336. For a recent book on ancient and ptolemaic Philae, see William MacQuitty, *Island of Isis: Philae, Temple of the Nile* (London, 1976). On Isis, see R.E. Witt, *Isis in the Graeco-Roman World* (London, 1971) esp. pp. 61–64.

'Monastic Egypt'. The farthest points south on it are Tabennesi and Phbow, two communities established by Saint Pachomius: this implies that monastic Egypt in the south was coterminus with pachomian Egypt.[118] Butler's map of 'Monastic Egypt. 400 AD' goes only as far south as Hermonthis and Latopolis.[119] When modern maps of christian and monastic Egypt do include Aswan and Philae, these are pictured at the very bottom of the map; looking at them, one imagines that if he had visited these towns at the end of the fourth century he would have been venturing dangerously close to the borders of the known world.[120]

This is probably also what a citizen of the fourth century felt. The *Life of Pachomius* reports that after Athanasius was elected archbishop of Alexandria, he 'came south to the Thebaid with the intention of proceeding as far as Aswan to give comfort to the holy churches'.[121] Apparently there was no one further south to be comforted, or if there was, Athanasius had no intention of seeking him out.

Athanasius was merely following precedent. The *Acts of the Martyrs* indicates that the emperors Diocletian and Maximilian 'established governors from Alexandria to Philae'.[122] And no further. The *Acts* also say that the emperors appointed governors 'from Rumania to Philae, outside of Egypt'.[123] Not only was Philae at the very border of Egypt, even outside of it, it stood on the border of the *oikoumene*, the known world.[124]

---

[118] Ward, *The Sayings of the Desert Fathers*. Veilleux, *Pachomian Koinonia* 1:489, includes Aswan at the far south of his map, but indicates that it lies outside the reach of pachomian monasticism, the furthest south of which (and last in order of founding) is Phnoum.

[119] Butler, 2:xcviii.

[120] See the maps in Chitty, following p. 96; Evetts and Butler, following p. 346; and Wolfgang Kosack, *Historisches Kartenwerk Ägyptens* (Bonn, 1971), Blatt 3 Oberägypten. For a good map of Syene (Aswan) and Philae in relation to the other churches of Egypt, see Karl Pieper, *Atlas Orbis Christiani Antiqui* (Düsseldorf, 1931) Map 8. A good modern map of the Nile region, with a detail of the Philae area, may be found in MacQuitty, pp. 20–21.

[121] *Vita Pachomii* 28; Veilleux, *A Pachomian Koinonia*, 1:51.

[122] H. Munier, 'Le Christianisme à Philae', *Bulletin de la société d'archéologie Copte* 4 (1938) 38.

[123] Ibid.

[124] The Coptic is ⲡⲓⲗⲁⲕϩ ⲉⲧⲥⲁⲃⲟⲗ ⲛⲧⲉⲭⲣⲙⲓ: Philae which is outside of Egypt. See Munier, 38. The first roman prefect in Egypt, Cornelius Gallus (29 BCE), fixed the border at Aswan; the meroitic kingdom to the south was admitted as a roman

The political boundary coincided with, and was probably partly the result of, a stark geographical divide between what lay north and south of the First Cataract. North of Aswan,

> the enclosing cliffs retreat for a distance from the river's edge. Between them, and stretching away to the horizon, lies the great valley which for millenia was practically synonymous with Egypt. The flat, incredibly green surface is marked off into squares and rectangles by rows of palm trees and by the glistening water of a thousand ditches and canals. . . .
> The view to the south offers a startling contrast. Here is no river valley; one might almost say no river. The Nile is lost to view almost at once among a tangle of rocky crests and slopes; even the dam, only a few miles away, is hidden from view. The green of vegetation and the yellow of desert sand—the two colors which dominate the landscape throughout Egypt proper—are alike missing as one looks south from Aswan. In their place appears nothing but the dull, dark grey of naked granite.
> No wonder, then, that Aswan marks the age-old frontier of Egypt's peasant civilization.[125]

The ancient name of Philae was Pi-lak, in Coptic ⲡⲓⲗⲁⲕϩ (*pi-lakh*), 'the corner', just above the head of the First Cataract. It was an island five hundred yards long and one hundred-sixty

---

protectorate. On the meroitic kingdom, see Adams, *Nubia*, pp. 338–9. See also Adams' earlier studies, 'Post Pharaonic Nubia in the Light of Archaeology. I, II, and III', *Journal of Egyptian Archaeology* 50 (1964) 102–120; 51 (1965) 160–178; and 52 (1966) 147–162. For a review of Adams' articles, see Bryan G. Haycock, 'The Later Phases of Meroitic Civilization', *Journal of Egyptian Archaeology* 53 (1967) 107–120. Further references in the present study to Adams' work will be to *Nubia*.

[125] Adams, p. 15. There is a picture of the island of Philae, taken before the building of the first Aswan dam, in Walter B. Emery, *Egypt in Nubia* (London, 1965) Plate II, following p. 128. Adams also comments, pp. 15–16, on the inhabitants south of the First Cataract: 'The land beyond the First Cataract offered few attractions either to farming or to commerce, and the ordinary Egyptian was happy enough to leave it in the hands of its immemorial occupants [the Nubians]: a hardy, brown-skinned race differing alike in appearance, in speech, and in custom from the Egyptians'.

yards wide, and consisted 'of a crystalline granite mixed with hornblende, beneath the alluvial deposits of the Nile'. Philae was located near latitude twenty-four (Alexandria is around latitude thirty-one), and it would have taken several days to get down to Alexandria by boat from Philae and much longer back against the current.[126] Abû Ṣâliḥ, a christian Armenian, traveled the Nile in the late twelfth century and recorded his observations:

> Between the land of Nubia and the land of the Muslims there are two stones upon a hill in the midst of the blessed river Nile; and the Muslims possess, opposite to them, a strong and lofty fortress called Philae... [which] contains fortified dwellings, and the ruins of well-built edifices, the works of the ancients. Philae is five miles distant from Aswan.[127]

Abû Ṣâliḥ describes Aswan as 'the large frontier-town and the great caravan station, and the last post of the Muslims [before you enter Nubia]'.[128] Aswan (*Syene* in Greek and Roman times)

> lies on the east bank [of the Nile], partly on the plain, and partly on a hill.... The fertile strip here is narrow, but supports numerous date-palms, the fruit of which enjoys a high reputation. The Nile divides into several arms, separated by granite rocks and islands, the largest of which is Elephantine. The horizon on the west is bounded by the Libyan hills, on the east by the Arabian mountains.... [It has an] equable and dry climate.[129]

Elephantine was strategically important to Rome because it commanded the Nile cataracts and waterways between Egypt and Nubia. Because of the caravan routes, the Aswan-Philae area was also important economically. For these reasons, the Ptolemies and later the Romans stationed troops here, and the region acted as a

---

[126]Karl Baedeker, *Egypt and the Sudan* (New York, 1929) 390. There is a map of Philae following p. 390 and a map of the temple of Isis on Philae. See also MacQuitty, p. 121. I am grateful to Birger A. Pearson for supplying the latitude figures.
[127]Evetts and Butler, pp. 274–5.
[128]Evetts and Butler, pp. 274–5.
[129]Baedeker, p. 379.

buffer between Egypt proper and Nubia: 'the northern extremity of Nubia between Syene (Aswan) and Pselcis (Dakkah)... was a dependency... called Dodecaschoenus'.[130]

To protect the frontier, regiments of *limitanei*—frontier soldiers—were stationed at Aswan and Philae:

> ...most of the propertied and literate male inhabitants of these towns were enrolled in their garrisons. The regiments are never named in the documents, but those of Syene and Philae are sometimes styled legions.... The legion of Philae was doubtless Legio I Maximiliana...that of Syene may have been the Milites Miliarii.[131]

Juvenal, the satiric poet (early second century), was made prefect of the garrison at Syene—or, in other words, as a punishment for his biting attacks, he 'was banished to the most remote frontier of the empire'.[132]

Aswan and Philae must have had the look of frontier towns, garrisoned and heavily fortified, a long, long way from Alexandria, and (for someone like Juvenal) infinitely remote from Rome. Frontier towns in the Roman Empire—as Dura-Europos in Syria bears witness—were in a precarious situation. In 25 BC Ethiopians had seized Syene, Elephantine, and Philae, defeating three roman cohorts.[133] Because of continuous harrassment from nomadic tribes, Diocletian drew the frontier back, from Hierasykaminos to Syene. He invited the Nobadae, a nomadic tribe, to settle in the Nile valley to act as a buffer against the Blemmyes, another

---

[130]Evetts and Butler, p. 260, n. 2. On Elephantine, see Adams, p. 336. Cornelius Gallus met with meroitic envoys at Philae; following this treaty, the Dodekaschoenus was administered as part of the southernmost nome of Egypt. See Adams, pp. 338–9, and p. 339, for a map of the Dodekaschoenus province. The Thebaid was made a separate province in 297; see A.H.M. Jones, *The Later Roman Empire 284–602* (Baltimore, 1986) 43. In 297 Diocletian 'withdrew the Roman garrisons and established the imperial frontier at Philae, leaving the Dodekaschoenus at the mercy of nomads'. See Adams, p. 389. E. Amélineau, *La géographie de l'Égypte à l'époque Copte* (Paris, 1893) 467–8, notes that Aswan is mentioned 'very frequently' in coptic documents.

[131]Jones, pp. 654–5, 662.

[132]Baedeker, p. 380.

[133]J. Grafton Milne, *A History of Egypt Under Roman Rule* (London, 1924) 9.

nomadic tribe. The Romans made payments to both tribes in an attempt to buy peace.[134] The treaty engineered by Diocletian at the end of the third century—along with considerable new fortifications and reinforcements—was to bring relative calm to the area until the time of Theodosius II (451).[135]

As frontier towns with large numbers of soldiers, Aswan and Philae must have shared in the syncretistic religious milieu of the Roman Empire in the hellenistic period.[136] At Philae, in fact, the religious importance of the temple of Isis dominated the administrative structure of government, not unlike the way cathedrals came to dominate their towns in the european Middle Ages.[137] Philae was referred to as 'the holy island', 'the interior of heaven', and 'the city of Isis'.[138] In practice, the island

> was a semi-autonomous buffer zone—a feudal principality administered by the priesthood of Isis as nominal vassals both of Egypt and of Nubia. In their inscriptions, the civil and even the military officials of Lower Nubia often designated themselves as 'Agents of Isis' rather than as servants of this or that Egyptian or Meroitic ruler.[139]

---

[134]Milne, p. 80. Pliny described the Blemmyes as a 'headless race whose eyes and ears do grow beneath their shoulders'. See Adams, p. 389, and pp. 419–422. In *Paralipomena* 9, a pachomian monk is mistreated by a band of Blemmyes; see Veilleux, *Pachomian Koinonia* 2:30–1. The Blemmyes of classical tradition are probably the same as the Beja tribes of today and the Medjay or Medju tribes mentioned in hieroglyphic texts from the Egyptian Middle Kingdom. See Adams, pp. 389 and 417. On the Blemmyes and Nobadae, see further Emery, pp. 232–238, and T.C. Skeat, 'A Letter from the King of the Blemmyes to the King of the Noubades', *Journal of Egyptian Archaeology* 63 (1977) 159–170.

[135]Diocletian doubled and tripled the troops under his command from the levels of the second and third century. See Milne, pp. 99, 179; Jones, p. 45.

[136]See Witt, plate 69, following p. 224, for a 'Coptic stele, from the Fayum, showing the mother and child—the basic iconography of Isis and Horus/Mary and Jesus'.

[137]For a good overview, with numerous pictures, of the transition from pagan to christian Egypt, see Alan K. Bowman, *Egypt after the Pharoahs* ([London]: University of California Press, 1986), 165–202.

[138]Adams, p. 337. Philae was also the 'pure island' where Isis dwelt; see L.V. Zabkar, 'Adaptations of Ancient Egyptian Texts to the Temple Ritual at Philae', *Journal of Egyptian Archaeology* 66 (1980) 128.

[139]Adams, p. 377.

The temple of Isis at Philae was as famous in antiquity as it was imposing in its dimensions.[140] Numerous inscriptions testify that 'Greek and Roman pilgrims flocked in crowds' to visit the shrine.[141] Not only Greeks and Romans, but the nomadic Nobadae of Nubia and Blemmyes of eastern Egypt worshiped here: as late as the sixth century these tribes enjoyed 'by treaty the right of annually borrowing the image of Isis from the temple of Philae'.[142] According to the historian Priscus, 'they would according to custom have free crossing to the temple of Isis. The Egyptians would have charge of the river boat for taking the statue to their own land and, having used it for the purpose of an oracle, bring it back to the island'.[143] Justinian (525–565) finally closed the temple and took the statue to Constantinople around 540.[144]

Isis was the chief deity worshiped at Philae, but Osiris and Hathor, along with the gods of the cataracts and other deities, were worshiped here also.[145] On the island there was a temple of Hathor as well as a temple of Trajan (the temple of Isis is pictured on a coin of Trajan).[146] Temple drawings of Claudius, Tiberius, Hadrian, and Trajan represent the roman emperors as egyptian

---

[140]See H. Leclercq, 'Philae', 692–703. For a detailed description of the temples, with maps and drawings, see H.G. Lyons, *A Report on the Temples of Philae* (Cairo, 1908). See Emery, Fig. 4, p. 36, for a map of Philae based on Lyons' map and, for a description of the temple, Witt, pp. 62–63. When the high dam was built at Aswan, the temple—which had already suffered damage from the dam built at the turn of the century—was moved to an island behind the dam. See A. Hoyt Hobbs and Joy Adzigian, *Fielding's Egypt and the Archaeological Sites* (New York, 1984), p. 208. Emery, p. 37, notes the destruction caused by the earlier dam on the '. . . maze of mud brick houses, churches and other buildings excavated at that time and of which we have little or no record. All were destroyed by the water of the reservoir when the Aswan dam was built, and with them went archaeological evidence of vital importance. . . .'

[141]Baedeker, p. 390; Leclercq, 698–703.

[142]This despite the edicts of Theodosius against pagan worship. See Jones, p. 942. *Paralipomena* 9 records the story of a pachomian monk being forced by the Blemmyes to sacrifice to their gods; see Veilleux, *Pachomian Koinonia* 2:30–1.

[143]Adams, p. 417.

[144]See Jones, p. 942, and Adams, p. 440.

[145]Baedeker, p. 390; Leclercq, 698–703.

[146]For pictures of the temple of Hathor, see Milne, pp. 3 and 14; Trajan, p. 238; the coin of Trajan, p. 209. See also Charles Coulston Gillispie and Michel Dewachter, eds., *Monuments of Egypt: The Napoleonic Edition. The Complete Archaeological Plates from La Description de L'Egypte* (Princeton, 1987) plates 1–29; and Robert Anderson and Ibrahim Fawzy, *Egypt Revealed: Scenes from Napoleon's La Description de l'Egypte* (Cairo, 1987) plates 1–2. For numerous pictures and a

pharoahs or gods.¹⁴⁷ An arch of Diocletian, as well as inscriptions and graffiti, shows the continuing importance of the island as a place of worship.¹⁴⁸

Although much of the island of Philae, especially the center and western portions, was dominated by temples, the northern part once showed the remains of two coptic churches and a coptic convent—as well as a ruined temple of Augustus.¹⁴⁹ As early as the end of the fourth century, upper Egypt was famous to Christians as a spiritual shrine, a place where God was at work in the world. As the *Historia Monachorum* recorded:

> What should one say about the Upper Thebaid in the district, where even more wonderful men are to be found and an infinite number of monks? One would not believe their ascetic practices which surpass human capabilities. To this day they raise the dead and walk on water just like Peter. And all that the Saviour did through the saints, he does in our times through these monks.¹⁵⁰

Abû Ṣâliḥ, eight hundred years later, visited the sites of these christian "shrines." The ruins he saw stood as silent witness to the effusive words of the *Historia Monachorum*: the saints were long dead, their churches and monasteries rubble, but Abû Ṣâliḥ poignantly noted their continuing presence: [There is in this district]

> a church named after the saint Abû Hadrî, whose body is preserved within it, but it is in ruins. It stands on the

---

good popular presentation of pre-christian worship on Philae, see MacQuitty, *Island of Isis*.

¹⁴⁷Milne, pp. 13, 15, 16, 20, 39, and 43.

¹⁴⁸Milne, p. 80. See also Ulrich Wilcken, 'Heidnisches und Christliches aus Ägypten. I: Das Christentum auf der Insel Philae', *Archiv für Papyrusforschung und verwandte Gebiete* 1 (1901) 396–7.

¹⁴⁹For a dramatic view of Philae and how the pagan temples dominated the island, see Lyons, plate IV, 'Philae Island', following p. 32. The main street of the coptic village ran through this area. The western of the two churches was the Church of Saint Mary. The extreme southwest corner of the island had coptic ruins. Kosack, Blatt 3 Oberägypten, indicates two destroyed churches each for Aswan and Philae.

¹⁵⁰*Historia Monachorum*, Epilogue; Russell, p. 118.

island of Ûswan [i.e., Elephantine]. Near this church there is also a monastery, in which there were three hundred cells for monks, which are now ruined. The church was large and beautiful.[151]

Who were the predecessors of these monks, these monastery- and church-builders? And when did they bring Christianity to Aswan and Philae?

Justinian closed the temple of Isis in the mid-sixth century, and had its cult statue hauled unceremoniously to Constantinople. The pronaos or fore-temple of the great temple of Isis was converted to a church dedicated to Saint Stephen and the Christians of Philae had a bishop, Theodore, who was to lead them during the second half of that century.[152] In the mid-fifth century an attempt to close the temple had led to armed intervention by the Nubians; the closing in 540 was seemingly accepted without protest.[153] By 550 Philae was a christian island.[154]

The writer of the *Historia Monachorum* believed that around the year 400 there was an 'infinite number of monks' in the upper Thebaid. If there was—and the *Historia* offers no eyewitness accounts of them—they co-existed with non-christian neighbors who were certainly in the vast majority. Isis, and her worshipers, dominated the island of Philae: Marinus, in the *Life of Proclus*, written around 486, wrote of the great egyptian god 'Isis, who is still honored throughout Philae'.[155] Does Marinus unintentionally acknowledge here that the god's hold on the island is slipping?

---

[151] Evetts and Butler, p. 276.

[152] Munier, 44; Adams, p. 440. Witt, p. 64, notes: 'Material from the temple buildings is visible in the Coptic church erected in later times near to the temenos wall in honour of the Christian Mother of God by the Abbot Bishop Theodore. On a block built into the wall of this church is a representation of the Egyptian goddess of Justice, Ma'et, offered seemingly by Augustus. . . . An inscription still survives to let us know that the cross has been and always will be victorious.'

[153] Adams, p. 440. On the evangelization of the Nubians in the fifth and sixth century, see Adams, pp. 440–1, and P. L. Shinnie, *Medieval Nubia*, Sudan Antiquities Service, Museum Pamphlet No. 2 (Khartoum, 1954).

[154] Munier, 44, states that by the end of the sixth century, the epigraphical evidence shows, paganism had definitely disappeared and the population was Christian. Letronne dates Christianity on Philae to after 550; but see Wilcken, 397.

[155] Ἴσιν τὴν κατὰ τὰς Φίλας ἔτι τιμωμένην; Leclercq, 694. The persistence of the Isis cult is testified to by Procopius and greek demotic inscriptions from the time of Diocletian to Justinian. See Wilcken, 397.

Corroboration for such a conjecture comes from a papyrus letter written by Appion, bishop of Syene, Kentrasyene, and Elephantine, which can be dated to 425–450.[156] Appion's diocese, it seems, is being invaded by marauders, so he appeals to the emperors Theodosius and Valentinian for military help. Bishop Appion terms Philae a *phrourion*, a garrisoned fort, and asks for help from the soldiers stationed nearby and from the garrison at Philae.[157] Appion also indicates that there are 'holy churches of God on Philae', and that the soldiers stationed on the island are prepared to come to their assistance.[158]

Appion does not include Philae in the list of churches under his jurisdiction, and it thus seems reasonable to infer that the churches in Philae were under the stewardship of another bishop.[159] Odd as

---

[156]Text in Wilcken, 399–400. On the dating, see Wilcken, 401–3. The following translation, with modifications by the present author, is that of Apostolos N. Athanassakis of the University of California at Santa Barbara.

'To Theodosius and Valentinian, eternal emperors, Flavian lords of earth and sea and of every human nation, [this is] a petition and a supplication [submitted] by Appion, Bishop of the [region] of Syene and of Kentrasyene and of Elephantine, [all of which] constitute an eparchy of [the] Upper Thebaid. Your compassion [*philanthropia*] has traditionally extended a helping hand to [all] petitioners. Fully aware of this, therefore, I have brought forward these petitions, whose subject is this: [I find myself] with my churches in the midst of impious barbarians, that is, between the Blemmyes and the Nobadae[. . . .]Since there is no soldier in charge of our territories, we are unable to withstand their attacks. For this reason[. . .]conditions are worsening for my churches and me and, since we are unable to offer protection even to those who take refuge with us, I kneel before you and prostrate myself at your pure and divine feet, that you might deem it worthy to order that my holy churches be guarded by your soldiers and that they [the soldiers] be commanded [. . .] to be alert to every [situation], just as the soldiers stationed in the camp at Philae—termed [an] 'outpost' [*phrourion*] of your Upper Thebaid—assist the holy churches of God on Philae. Thus, we shall be able to live without fear and to avail ourselves of the strictest laws against the offenders [. . .] [laws, that is,] passed by you [. . .] and [. . .] of pillaging perpetrated by those [residing] in enemy territory [. . .] of your divine [. . .] and [. . .] special favor regarding this matter conferred upon the magnificent and distinguished governor and leader of the eparchy of [the] Thebaid. If, as is your custom, you grant this, I pray to God that he bestow upon you eternal life for ever'.

We know from the pachomian sources that monks lived near the Blemmyes, and did not think kindly of them. See Paralipomena 9 in Armand Veilleux, *Pachomian Koinonia*, 2, *Pachomian Chronicles and Rules* (Kalamazoo, 1981) 30–31.

[157]Wilcken, 400. Appion designates Philae thus: καθὼς οἱ φίλῳ Κάστρα καλουμένῳ φριορίῳ τῆς ὑμέτερας [sic] Ἄνω Θηβαίδος καταστᾰθέντες στρατιῶται. . . .

[158]Wilcken, 400.

[159]Wilcken, 401.

it may seem to us today, Philae may have had its own bishop at this time precisely because it was a *phrourion*. Military stations in Egypt, 'though they might technically lie in a city territory, were probably separately administered and had a life of their own'. These camps 'tended to become bishoprics'.[160] The fact that Philae at this time was a garrison town, had at least two churches, and was not under the jurisdiction of the bishop of Syene, strongly suggests that in the second quarter of the fifth century it had its own bishop.

The evidence presented by Appion's letter also indicates that in the fifth century Christians and non-christians on Philae lived near one another: the non-christians to the south and center of the island, where the great temples were, and the Christians to the north, where archeological evidence shows that there were churches.[161] Christians and non-christians (including Jews) in Egypt lived side by side (or at least near) one another for centuries, and it certainly seems reasonable to suppose that they did so in the upper Thebaid on the island of Philae.

If the Christians did have several churches and a bishop at Philae in the first half of the fifth century, when had they first come to the island? Paphnutius' *Histories of the Monks of Upper Egypt* suggests an answer. Abba Isaac, apparently a native of the region, sat at the feet of Abba Aaron, and thus embodies several generations of local tradition. He tells Paphnutius about the first bishops of Philae (pars. 29–85): Macedonius, a Christian, sometime in the mid-fourth century (330–370) was made a local governor, possibly of Aswan or of the entire upper Thebaid (par. 29; the text, unfortunately, is badly preserved here). One day he visits Philae; since it is the sabbath day he desires to attend worship but cannot because the Christians are few, they live in fear of the non-christians, and they have no church. A resident of Philae tells Macedonius that clergy from Aswan come and administer the sacraments to them.

Later, on a trip to Alexandria, Macedonius pays a visit to Bishop Athanasius and asks him to appoint a bishop for Philae. The bishop replies, in effect, 'Who better than you?' and ordains Macedonius

---

[160]Jones, p. 878. He instances Philae, Syene and Elephantine, Babylon, and Scenae Mandron.

[161]This is also Wilcken's conclusion, 402–3. See the map 'Philae Island', plate IV, following p. 32 in Lyons. Munier, 44, accepts Wilcken's suggestion. On the ancient churches at Philae, see Leclercq, 697, and on the christian epigraphy at the temple of Isis, 698–703.

the first bishop of the island.¹⁶² Macedonius returns south, destroys an image of a falcon worshiped locally, and converts the two sons of the temple priest. Eventually the temple priest is also converted and baptized, and Macedonius then baptizes the entire city. The sons of the temple priest, now Macedonius' 'sons', whom he christens Mark and Isaiah, become a priest and a deacon; they eventually succeed Macedonius as bishops of Philae.

Surely, one might argue, this is all legendary.¹⁶³ It is too neat. And why the statue of a falcon and not the statue of the great Isis herself? The story, however, does bear further examination. If Philae had a christian community with a bishop sometime around 425–450 (see above, p. 63), then that community could certainly have had its beginning during the episcopacy of Athanasius (328–373), the time suggested by the narrative of Paphnutius. The history of the bishops of Philae places the fourth bishop, Pseleusias, at the beginning of the episcopacy of Theophilus of Alexandria (385), and it seems that Paphnutius made his visit to Philae while Pseleusias was bishop, sometime between 390–400 (see p. 53 above). Some of the details of the story about Macedonius also have historical credibility: when Macedonius first comes to the island, it is overwhelmingly non-christian; the few Christians there are afraid to worship openly and are ministered to by clergy from Aswan, which would have been likely.

Despite these plausabilities, if all we had was the information from Paphnutius' *Histories*, we would be hard pressed to reach a conclusion about the first bishops of Philae. Evidence outside of Paphnutius' *Histories*, however, goes far to corroborate several important details. Athanasius, in a letter dated to 362, gives the names of bishops attending a council in Alexandria: one of these bishops is 'Mark of Philae' (Μάρκος Φιλῶν).¹⁶⁴ We know from Paphnutius that a Mark succeeded Macedonius, and 362 is certainly a plausible

---

¹⁶²This story accurately reflects the power of the bishop of Alexandria; see Annick Martin, 'Aux origines de l'église copte: L'implantation et le developpement du christianisme en Égypte (Ie–IVe siècles)', *Revue des Études Anciennes* 83/1 (1981) 45–6.

¹⁶³So states Leclercq, 697; Munier, 41, believes that the story of Macedonius is 'certainly legendary', but 'retains a certain historical base'.

¹⁶⁴See Wilcken, 404; Wilhelm Spiegelberg, 'Der Falkonkultus auf der Insel Philae in christlicher Zeit', *Archiv für Papyrusforschung und verwandte Gebiete* 7 (1924) 188–9; Munier, 42.

date for his episcopacy. Before the publication of the *Histories*, objection was made to the evidence offered by Athanasius on two grounds: (1) Philae at that time was not christian, and (2) with the exception of Mark, only bishops from lower Egypt signed the document. The text, it was suggested, should read Μάρκος Σίλων, thus placing Mark in a village in lower Egypt.[165]

Emendation should be a measure of last resort; one bishop on Athanasius' list was from the Fayum in upper Egypt.[166] Before the publication of Paphnutius' *Histories*, one had to rely on the letter of Bishop Appion to the roman emperors to argue that Christianity should be placed at Philae earlier than scholars had previously thought, but that the date could be no earlier than 425.[167] With the evidence that Athanasius' letter offers, and the chronology Paphnutius presents, it now seems reasonable to place Macedonius as the first christian bishop of Philae, sometime around 350–360.[168]

Macedonius' first act as bishop of Philae, according to Paphnutius, was to invade a pagan temple dedicated to a falcon cult and destroy the 'idol' within. This is not improbable: Theophilus, bishop of Alexandria, had the Serapeum in Alexandria destroyed in 391 and the great monastic leader Shenoute was famous (or infamous) for his destruction of idols.[169] A story in the *Historia Monachorum* is strikingly similar to that about Macedonius. In it Apollo, a christian holy man living in Hermopolis in the Thebaid, drives non-christian worship out of his neighborhood:

---

[165] The arguments were made by Letronne; see Spiegelberg, 188–9 and Wilcken, 401–4. Leclercq, 697, accepts the emendation of the text.

[166] Wilcken, 404. Spiegelberg, 188–9, following Wilcken, accepts Mark's name in the list as is and rejects Letronne's objections.

[167] As Wilcken did. The argument that Mark could not be a bishop at Philae in 362 because that is too early a date for Christianity in Philae is circular. Leclercq, 697, doubts that there could be a bishop this early at the farthest extremes of upper Egypt. Munier, however, correctly points out, 41, that the evangelization of Egypt was not systematic. On the widespread christian presence throughout Egypt by the time of the Council of Nicea, see Martin, 35–56. Martin believes, 42 and 44, that persecution and monasticism were two of the main causes of the expansion of Christianity in the third and fourth centuries. He does not discuss Aswan and Philae or Paphnutius' writings.

[168] Macedonius' Greek name was not unusual for a fourth-century bishop; see Martin, 48–50.

[169] Abba Bessarian said to John of Lycopolis: 'A decree has gone out that the temples should be destroyed'. See Chitty, p. 54. For Shenoute, see David N. Bell, tr., *Besa: The Life of Shenoute* (Kalamazoo, 1983) 83–84; p. 66.

> For there were once pagans living near him in all that region, and the neighboring villages in particular practiced the idolatrous worship of demons. There was a huge temple in one of the villages which housed a very famous idol, though in reality this image was nothing but a wooden statue. The priests together with the people, working themselves up in a bacchic frenzy, used to carry it in procession through the villages, no doubt performing the ceremony to ensure the flooding of the Nile.

Apollo stops their worship, converts the villagers, and together they burn the idol: 'As a body they all rushed towards him, committing themselves fully to belief in the Saviour of the universe and the God who works miracles, and at once set fire to the idol'.[170]

The story of the destruction of the idol at Philae and the conversion of its priest and of all the non-christians on the island was probably taken by the Christians of Philae—a minority, certainly—as a sign of the triumph of Christianity, perhaps more eschatalogical than actual. The conversion of the island must have proceeded much more slowly than this: during the fifth century, as we have seen, Christians and non-christians shared the island, and Christianity was not to triumph until the middle of the sixth century.[171]

The destruction of *one* idol, even though a dangerous act, was much more possible. The historian and geographer Strabo (64 BC-c. 21 AD) testifies in fact to the worship of a bird (ὄρνεον) on Philae which the natives, he says, call a falcon (ἱέρακα).[172] Late hieroglyphic temple inscriptions at Philae show that a falcon (bjk, Coptic ⲃⲏϭ) was worshiped at Philae as a bird sacred to the god of light, as the 'spirit of Re'.[173] Strabo does not mention Isis, or any other of the cults on the island. Nor does Paphnutius.[174] A reason

---

[170]Russell, tr., pp. 73–4.

[171]On non-christian resistance to christianization in the fourth century, see Roger Rémondon, 'L'Égypte et la suprême résistance au christianisme', *Bulletin de l'Institut Français d'Archéologie Orientale du Caire* 51 (1952) 63–78. Ewa Wipszycka, 'La christianisation de l'Égypte aux IVe–VIe siècles. Aspects sociaux et ethniques', *Aegyptus* 68 (1988) 142–58, shows the strong presence that paganism had well into the fifth century.

[172]Spiegelberg, 187.

[173]Spiegelberg, 187. In Aswan, as late as the twelfth century, there was 'an

for this is not immediately apparent, but Strabo's testimony makes less extraordinary the fact that Paphnutius does not mention the famous Isis or any other deities.

Before 1900, scholars placed the christianization of Philae in the mid-sixth century. The discovery of the letter by Bishop Appion of Aswan makes it possible to push that date back to the time of Theodosius II, around 450. Because of the letter of Athanasius mentioning Mark and the evidence Paphnutius offers, which is corroborated at several important points by witnesses outside of the text, I suggest a date of c. 350 for the first bishop of Philae.[175] That there were Christians already there, as the *Histories* suggests, seems likely, even though it is not possible at this point to determine when they came.[176]

Paphnutius, I also suggest, is trustworthy. If he is not (or does not seem to be) historically accurate in every detail (the stories about the bishops of Philae do contain a good deal of legendary material), nevertheless he can be trusted with regard to the chronology of the bishops of Philae and the narrative concerning Abba Aaron. The history of the bishops of Philae told to Paphnutius is firmly founded in local history, and was very probably

---

ancient temple, containing the figure of a scorpion' which had magical powers. See Evetts and Butler, p. 275.

[174]Spiegelberg, 188. Diodore, Procopius, and Servius do mention the other gods.

[175]Spiegelberg, 188, and Munier, 41, were willing to place Christianity at Philae around 400.

[176]There is one opposing piece of evidence to my suggestions. Eutychius reports in his *Annales* (*Patrologia Graeca* 111:1005) that a bishop of Philae, an Arian by the name of Eusebius during the time of Bishop Alexander of Alexandria (311–328), accompanied Arius to see Constantine in 324: 'Cum ergo Alexander patriarcha Alexandrinus, Arium Ecclesiane ingredi prohiberet, eique malediceret. Profectus ille ad Constantinum imperatorem opem ab ipso contra Alexandrinum patriarcham petiit. Comites autem se Ario praebuerunt episcopi duo, quorum unus nomine Eumenius [al. Eusebius], Nicomediae episcopus, alter Eusebius Philae episcopus, opem a Constantino implorantes'. Eutychius, however, is not trustworthy, and is prone to use legendary material. As one modern historian has objected: '. . . Eutychius is so reckless and ignorant a writer that nothing can be taken for history because Eutychius says it'. It is difficult to see how Eutychius' report could have any validity. See Tim Vivian, *Saint Peter of Alexandria: Bishop and Martyr* (Philadelphia, 1988), p. 14 and n.27, and Gedaliahu G. Stroumsa, 'The Manichaean Challenge to Egyptian Christianity,' in Birger A. Pearson and James E. Goehring, eds., *The Roots of Egyptian Christianity* (Philadelphia, 1986) 312, n.24.

a local account of the early days of Christianity in Philae. This history is largely monastic, and that too is not surprising, and seems reasonable.[177]

The story of Abba Aaron as told to Paphnutius by Isaac appears to be the first-hand account by a disciple who had sat at the feet of the master. Its many small details and observations give it the ring of truth; its trenchant observations about the rich are at once local and universal. There are miracles, which may or may not be 'true': one cannot simply dismiss them. The scenes and customs of local life are so sharply observed and clearly presented that it is evident we are hearing from a native and an eyewitness to the events being related.

These two parts of Paphnutius' *Histories of the Monks of Upper Egypt* are valuable for the study of early christian Egypt: the history of the bishops of Philae allows us to place Christians on the island from the middle of the fourth century; the 'Life of Abba Aaron' (as well as the *Life of Onnophrius*) tells us about the spirituality of some of these citizens of God. Their stories are still worth listening to.

THE MANUSCRIPTS

The translations in this volume are based on the Coptic texts published by E.A. Wallis Budge in volumes IV and V of *Coptic Texts*. The text of 'The Life of Apa Onnophrius, the Anchorite' is found in volume IV, pp. 205–224; the text of the '[Histories of the Monks in the Upper Egyptian Desert by Paphnutius]' is in volume V pt. 1, pp. 432–495. Because the manuscript of the *Histories* is damaged and has numerous lacunae, I have checked Budge's text against a microfilm from the British Library and have made the appropriate changes in my translation wherever necessary.

The manuscript of the *Histories of the Monks of Upper Egypt* is now found in the British Library, Oriental 7029. Budge gives a description of the manuscript in volume V, pp. lvi-lix. Pictures of this manuscript may be found in plates XXXII–XXXVIII following p. 1216 in *Coptic Texts*, vol. V pt. 2. Ms Oriental 7029 is item #163 in Bentley Layton's recent *Catalogue of Coptic*

---

[177]Bishop Theodore, in the mid-sixth century, was apparently a monk. See Witt, p. 64.

Literary Manuscripts in the British Library (pp. 196–8). Layton gives a description of the manuscript and a summary of the contents of the *Histories*; he dates Oriental 7029 to the year 992 or 982. Layton discovered that, unbeknownst to Budge, another manuscript in the British Library contains three small fragments of the *Histories*: Oriental 7558 (89) (93) (150). These fragments are listed under item #150 in Layton's catalogue (pp. 172–3); on p. 173 he gives the approximate correspondence to Oriental 7029.

The *Life of Onnophrius* on which the present translation is based is also found in the Oriental collection of the British Library, and is manuscript Oriental 7027. Budge supplies a description of this manuscript in *Coptic Texts* vol. IV: pp. xxi–xxii; plates XX–XXVI following p. 523 show the manuscript, and plates XX–XXIV picture selections from the *Life of Onnophrius*. Layton lists Oriental 7027 as item #161 in his catalogue, and dates it to 1004. On pp. 192–3 he gives a description of the manuscript and a summary of the contents. The manuscript is intact.

Unlike the *Histories of the Monks of Upper Egypt*, the *Life of Onnophrius* by Paphnutius has survived in a number of manuscripts in Sahidic and Bohairic Coptic and in Arabic and Latin. There exists also a 'Discourse on Onnophrius' attributed to Pisenthius.[178] D.S. Chauler, in his article 'Saint Onuphre', discusses the various texts of the life of Onnophrius and provides on p. 13 a bibliography of the published and unpublished manuscripts. The only unedited Coptic text is Codex Pierpont Morgan M. 580, Vol. 48.[179] Not included in Chauler's bibliography are fragments published by Tito Orlandi and L.Th. Lefort which these scholars believe to be more ancient witnesses to the text. For their works, consult the bibliography in this volume.

---

[178]Because this 'Discourse' (a sermon really) is fragmentary and because, in my estimation, it contains nothing about the historical Paphnutius, I have chosen not to translate it for this work. For the Coptic text and a French translation, see W.E. Crum, 'Discours de Pisenthius sur Saint Onnophrius', *Revue de l'Orient Chrétien*, 2nd series 10 (20) (1915–17), 38–67.

[179]For a translation of this text, see Tim Vivian, 'The *Life of Onnophrius*: A New Translation', *Coptic Church Review* 12/4 (Winter 1991) 99–111.

HISTORIES OF THE MONKS OF UPPER EGYPT

I. PAPHNUTIUS VISITS WITH PSELEUSIUS AND THE BRETHREN[1]

1. / [. . . .][2] and the service[3] which we have entrusted to you. Blessed are we! Our land [has] become worthy of your holy footsteps. The psalmist David rightly said: *Beloved are [your] habitations,* and again, *Beloved are they on account of their fathers.* It is the Lord who [speaks], for [. . .] with great [fear?] and gladness.[4] I remember what the Lord said in the Gospel: *In the house which you enter, first of all say, 'Peace be with this house.' If there are children of peace there, let your peace rest upon it. If not, let your peace [return] to you.* When I found that they were children of peace, I allowed my peace to rest upon them, according to the word of the teacher of us all, Christ Jesus our Lord.

2. Now, when the time had come, we celebrated the eucharist.[5] A table was prepared for us, and we prayed. We ate [and we drank. . . .] / ate with these holy ones of God, as did the servant of Abraham who was joyfully [brought in], and all their desires were fulfilled. I [too] glorified God because he did not [. . .] the one who seeks

/Fol. 1a

Ps 83:1, Septuagint [LXX]

Mt 10:12–13

/1b

Gen 24:33, 54

---

[1] Paragraphing and section titles are the present translator's.
[2] The first page or two are missing.
[3] Greek [Gr]: *diakonia.*
[4] The coptic text of this sentence is very uncertain.
[5] Gr: *synaxis.*

him. As it is written: 'The one who [...] people, fulfills the worship of God'.[6] After we had lighted the lamp, we completed our [prayer], praying and talking [about] the word of God and the holy teachings.

3. Then I spoke with the holy old man, Abba Pseleusius, about a certain master, a good brother with whom <he>[7] had lived, that is, Abba Zebulon. He was a man whose company you could profit from, and we profited greatly from him. He said to me, 'I myself profited from him in this way: I benefitted from his humility and silence. He refused to [decide] with words any matter whatsoever. Whether the person who spoke with him was unimportant or whether he was great, he always said, "[I do not] know"'.

The Story of Abba Pseleusius

4. I said to him, 'How [is it that you can speak] /2a in this way [and] / act thus?' The old man said to [me]: 'Listen, and I will tell [you]. In his youth Pseleusius took to himself a wife, and he made progress in every work. He was a virgin from his childhood, and he fled from all intercourse with women because he was afraid of what is written: *Whoever looks upon a woman to desire her has already committed adultery with her in his heart*, and *Desire,*

Mt 5:28; *when it has conceived, gives birth to death.* He walked
Jm 1:15 in complete humility, and he saw a vision in this way: As though he saw a glorious man standing before him, saying, "*No one can serve two masters.*
Mt 6:24; *Either he loves one or hates one.* This is exactly your
Lk 16:13 situation, my brother Pseleusius. You are zealous in good works, as it is written by the Apostle: *No one who is a soldier gets himself entangled in [civilian*

---

[6]The text is uncertain here, as is the location of the Scripture being cited.
[7]Text: you.

pursuits, since his aim is to satisfy] / the one who made him a soldier. Moreover, if one competes as an athlete, he does not receive a crown unless he competes according to the rules. You will be victorious on the right hand and on the left." And suddenly the one who was speaking with him disappeared and he no longer saw him.

5. 'Close by him lived a certain old man who was knowledgeable in the Scriptures. Pseleusius would often go to him and would inquire of him concerning the passages of Scripture read in church. (He loved the poor very much.) Moreover, he would often tell him his thoughts and satisfy his heart with the holy Scriptures. When morning came, he went to him and told him the vision he had seen and asked what it was intended to mean. The old man told him, "Part with everything you own, take up your cross, follow your Lord, and let the dead bury their dead. [. . .] / vain. Have you not heard the Lord crying out in the Gospels: *No one who puts his hand to the plow and then turns back is directed toward the kingdom of heaven?* Now this phrase 'look back' represents the cares for this vain world and its earthly concerns which we do not recognize.⁸ Now, then, my beloved brother, because your knowledge and your coming to me benefit me, I do not want to make you go and leave me, yet I do want you to walk in the calling to which you have been called. Rise, and go to the brethren, and they will clothe you in the habit of the monk, and they will tell you what is fitting for you to do."

/2b

2 Tim 2:4–5

Cf. Mt 8:22
/3a

Cf. Lk 9:62

Pseleusius Meets John

6. 'And so Pseleusius departed, as the old man had told him. He went to the brethren in a place

---

⁸Luke has 'look back', which is being exegeted here, while the coptic text cited above has 'turn back.'

called [...and met a monk whose] name [was /3b John....] / and very polite. His face was very pallid,[9] and his whole body even more so on account of his asceticism. As it is written: *The wings of a pigeon pale like silver, and round about* Ps 68:13 *her neck green as gold.* He speaks this way because when the old man raised up his hands, they were like the wings of a pigeon as described in the Scriptures. He likened him to the brilliance of silver on account of the purity of his prayers, and to the pale-green color of gold on account of the pallor caused by his asceticism. As it is written: *Blessed are the holy in heart, for they are the ones who* Mt 5:8 *will see God.* He was a laborer in suffering. He would often pass the night in vigil, and often he would eat wild plants as did John the Baptist, of whom it is testified: *[His food was locusts] and wild* Mt 3:4 *honey* [....] / because of his purity of heart and /4a his purity of body.'

Pseleusius Tells the Story of John

7. 'The holy father Abba Pseleusius said that he often saw numerous revelations and that every word he spoke would come true. He would see visions like Daniel the seer. Abba Pseleusius also said: "When, therefore, I had come to him—that is, to John about whom I first spoke and about whom I have said these things—he received me with great hospitality. I found nothing in his dwelling except three loaves of bread, and they were there only for strangers who should pass by, so it would not be said, "The old man does not eat bread." '

8. After I had stayed with him a while I entreated him to clothe me in the monastic habit /4b [...and teach me] / the monastic rules. And he

---

[9]Pallid: literally, 'green'. See the next sentence.

said to me, 'My brother Pseleusius, it is written: *Your words are sweeter in my throat, Lord, than honey in my mouth*. Since you have asked me, my son, about instruction, show propriety in the presence of outsiders, and be seasoned with salt as the Saviour says to his apostles in the Gospel: *You are the salt of the earth*. Be gentle and sincere in heart, as our Lord says: *Look, I am sending you as sheep in the midst of wolves. Therefore, be wise as these serpents and harmless as these doves*. He said to them, *like sheep*, but because of their carelessness he did not trust the sheep enough to make them walk in [. . . .] their hearts because of the wiles of the demons [. . . .] / destruction, nor to give ourselves over to eating and drinking and pleasure, for our adversary the Devil walks about laying traps for people, roaring like a lion, seeking to swallow our souls'.

Ps 119:103

Mt 5:13

Mt 10:16

/5a

Cf. 1 P 5:8

9. While I spent some days with him he [said] these words and others like them to me. I entreated him to take me to a place by myself, and so he brought me here. He stayed with me[10] some days until he had taught me how to live by myself in the desert, having given me certain commands and instructions how to resist the thoughts of the demons and wage the bitter fight against them.

10. He left me alone until my brother Zebulon came to me. Then he said to me, 'I entreat you, my father Pseleusius, since there is [. . . .]' / The old man responded and said to me, 'Since you have asked, I will tell you, and nothing will be kept from you. What is more, the Holy Spirit will reveal to you the things which are hidden from you before me.' I said to him, 'Please, my father, do not pass your servant by.' He answered, saying to me, 'Since you have asked, I will tell you.'

/5b

---

[10]The text has 'us'.

The Story of How John Meets Anianus and Paul

11. Abba John said: I went once into the further desert. After journeying about two days I found a few date palms in a little valley with a spring of water and some plants round about it. I sat down beside the spring to rest myself a little, worn out from my travels, and I said, 'I wonder whether or not there is a brother here.' Now, while I was pondering this, I looked up and saw /6a [two] men [. . . I] call[ed to them. . . .] / palm trees, and they brought me a little water to drink. I wanted to stay with them there, but I remembered my brother Zebulon. I could not remain without him, as the Apostle says: *When a great door was opened to me by [the Lord], I could not rest in my spirit <without> Titus my brother.* And again: *I have planted, it is Apollos who has watered, it is God who has given the growth.* And I said to them, 'How is it that you have come to this place, and what have you found to eat? What are your names and where are you from? How do you participate in the eucharist while you are here?'

2 Cor 2:12–13

1 Cor 3:6

The Story of Anianus and Paul

12. And they said: We are citizens of Aswan where we have lived since we were born. Moreover, we were friends: we would go to church together every day morning and evening and we'd listen to the holy Scriptures being read, and the reading from the Gospel which says: *Whoever loves /6b father or mother more than me / is not worthy of me. And whoever does not take up his cross and follow me is not worthy of me.*

Mt 10:37
Mt 10:38

13. Now when we heard these words of life from the mouth of our Lord and Saviour Jesus Christ, the lover of humanity, and words similar

to them[11]—that is, *Whoever loves [his] life will lose it, and whoever [loses] his life for my sake will find it,* and again: *If a person gains the whole world but forfeits his life, [what shall it profit him], or what shall a person give in exchange for his life?*—when we heard these things, our hearts were of one accord because the word of God was sweeter to us than honey in the honeycomb. We agreed together to leave the city on a certain day. Now, we waited a few days, saying, 'Perhaps demons are tempting us'. But when we perceived that a good intention was encouraging us not to give up our plan, we distributed our excess belongings among the needy and took a little boat and came to the monastic community,[12] a place called 'the corner'.

Cf. Jn 12:25;
Mt 10:39
Mt 16:26

14. We were able to live with the holy brothers in that place because by the grace of God it was a time of great plenty. We met a certain holy old man by the name of Zacchaeus who had grown old as an anchorite. He was a great ascetic. There were two other brothers living close by him, disciples of his. The name of one was Serapamon and the name of the other was Matthew. They were greatly advanced as spiritual athletes who gave thanks to God and obeyed the old man, Abba Zacchaeus, in everything that he told them.

The Ascetic Practices of Serapamon and Matthew

15. [Now] Serapamon had nurtured an act of love which was this: Whenever someone would come seeking to buy some handiwork from him, he would first gather the brethren and say to them, 'Whoever has any handiwork ready, bring it to

---

[11]The text has 'it' or 'him'.
[12]Or: mountain.

/7b me, [and I will] pay him his price'. And he would [...] the handiwork and eagerly [...] handiwork [...] / came to him, and he knew, because he would take it from him by force and give him his own. Moreover, he loved loss more than gain and shame more than honor. He continued in this act of love until the day of his perfection.

16. Now Matthew himself nurtured this ascetic practice:[13] He could never be persuaded to speak about any saying from Scripture, and if anyone asked him about a reading from [the] Scriptures, he would answer them in this way: 'Forgive me in this way, I do not understand it', [even] though he was very learned and had been instructed in the writings of the holy scriptures.[14] And thus he went to his rest on the fifteenth of Paone.[15]

The Ascetic Practices of Abba Zacchaeus

17. Now as for the old man, of whom we have already spoken, that is, Abba Zacchaeus, it was he who taught us how to live in the [desert] and it was he who clothed us in [the] monastic habit. The old man spoke with us also about the virtues[16] [of] the holy ones in the desert who zealously sought to see no one. He gave [us the rules] for a strict ascetic practice [...] and would command us, [saying], 'Take care for your souls!' /8a [...] / He was advanced in a very strict way of life,[17] despite his old age. He had been a virgin all of his life, and fled all intercourse with women and all conversation.

---

[13] *Politeia.*
[14] There is a play on words in the Coptic: 'learned' in Coptic is *sah* (ⲥⲁϩ); 'writings' is *shai* (ⲥϩⲁⲓ).
[15] June 22.
[16] Gr: *aretē.*
[17] *Politeia.*

Abba Zacchaeus Interprets the Holy Scriptures

18. Abba Zacchaeus loved tears more than laughter, and did not stop weeping day or night, so one day we said to him, 'My father, why do you weep this way?'

19. He said: 'It is fitting for one to perform all acts of renunciation and not to cease doing them day or night, weeping for his sins. As it is written: *Blessed are those who mourn, for they shall be comforted.* If you take this passage to heart, you will find relief from your sufferings. For it is right that all persons keep before them these three / things, namely their departure from the body, mindfulness of the decree which will be ours on the great and fearful day of judgement— for surely you have heard about the great Moses, how when he kept his hands raised, both of them, he would overcome Amalek, and how when he dropped them Amalek defeated / [the Israelites] and held power over them. For holy Scripture says that Aaron raised up the right hand of Moses and Hur the left. And thus, by their acting in concord and together raising up Moses' hands, Amalek was defeated. Holy Scripture also says, *And Aaron raised up his hands until evening,* that is, he stood the entire day.   Mt 5:4   /sic   /8b   Ex 17:11–13   Ex 17:12

20. 'So it is with humankind. Every person who lifts up his hands as a type of the cross of Christ defeats all his enemies, as did Moses who defeated Amalek by raising up his hands. As for Aaron, scripture likens him to the place of rest which is in heaven, and to the rejoicing which is in the heavenly Jerusalem, and to the throne and the robes which will be put upon the holy ones. As it is written: *You have torn off my sackcloth; you have clothed me with joy.* And again: *<He> shall be worthy to be a partner with the first-born whose names are written in heaven and in the / paradise in*   Ps 30:11   /9a

the east. Eye has not seen nor ear heard, neither has it entered the human heart, what God has prepared for those who love him.

<small>Cf. Heb 12:22–23
1 Cor 2:9,
Is 64:4</small>

21. 'Now Hur, for his part, Scripture likens to the judgements and to the worm that never sleeps and to the flood of tears, to the gnashing of teeth and the outer darkness, to the bottomless pit and the river of fire that flows fearfully. For when someone remembers these things in his heart whenever he prays, his petition advances to the throne of God and everything he asks from God will be granted him. As it is written: *The petition [of] a righteous person has great power and effect*, and it defeats the hidden Amalek and his power.

<small>Cf. Mt 8:12; Mk 9:48</small>

<small>Jm 5:16</small>

22. 'And the second thing one prays for is joy and weeping: joy because of weeping and the remembrance of the place of rest in heaven; weeping because of the remembrance of the punishments in hell (Amente). / [My brethren, my sons,] it is right for [all] persons to set before themselves the remembrance of these two things: rest and suffering. Thus, when we have suffered a little in this life, there will be rest.

<small>/9b</small>

Abba Zacchaeus Instructs Anianus and Paul

23. 'Now when we had heard these things from the holy old man, Abba Zacchaeus, we were filled [with] joy and we said to him, "Show [mercy] to us and take us to dwell where you know we will be saved". And so he gave us bread and two books. He journeyed with <us>[18] until he brought us to that place. He remained with us a few days until we knew how to live in the desert. He gave us some strict injunctions and rules regarding night vigils and responsible eating and drinking. And

---

[18]Text: them.

he taught us how the demons tempt people in various guises. As it is written by the Apostle: *The fight for us is not against flesh and blood but against the principalities, against the powers, against / the spirits of evil under heaven,* for the demons fight naked against each other at night. And he gave us certain rules so that if certain brothers came to us, we were to fight with them.

/10a
Eph 6:12

The Death of Abba Zacchaeus

24. 'And so he left us, and went to his rest on the eleventh of Thoth, and we have remained here to this day, our holy father.[19] Our food has been these date palms and we go forth to the outer monastery[20] and participate in the eucharist with the brothers on the Sabbath and the Lord's Day. Now we have told you about our withdrawal from the world. For your part, please do us the favor of praying for us, our holy father.

The Death of Anianus and Paul

25. 'So I left them and went to live in my own dwelling. The name of one of them was Anianus, and the name of the other was Paul. Now within a few days we heard from a brother who was in the habit of often visiting them. He found when he asked about them that both of them had gone to their rest, Anianus on the twentieth, / and Paul on the third, of Paope.[21] When our brother Banouphiel heard this, he went and got their bodies and buried them in a place near him.

/10b

---

[19] 21 September.
[20] Or: mountain.
[21] 13 October.

II. HISTORY OF THE BISHOPS OF PHILAE

The Story of Abba Isaac

26. 'Now then, my brother Paphnutius, I have told you these things concerning those who live in the desert—what I have seen and heard and remembered of the fathers who went before them and of their perfection. There remains that which I have to say about the holy old man, Abba Isaac, of blessed memory,[22] who had governed his way of life before he became a monk here. He lived on the island in the middle of the cataract, about four miles south of us.[23] He himself was a disciple of the holy old man Abba Aaron, and he poured water on his hands just as the great Elisha did for the prophet Elijah. He was in truth a man perfected in many different virtues.'

2 Kgs 3:11

Paphnutius and Pseleusius Go To Meet Isaac

27. When I heard of the blessedness of this man and the qualities he possessed, I entreated my father / Pseleusius, '[I will go] to him, and I will make myself worthy of his blessing. [And] thus we will pray in his dwelling.' And so we departed and embarked in a little boat and sailed south to find the holy old man Abba Isaac. Now there were huge rocks lying in the water in the middle of the river, and the waters there roared in a terrifying manner. And when we had gone south, we put ashore at the old man's dwelling. He had been informed by the Spirit of our landing a little earlier, and he came out and stood on the shore of the river. He was a man filled with grace and advanced in years. Now when we had

/11a

---

[22]This seems to be the correct translation, despite the problem of chronology suggested by the narrative.
[23]The island of Philae.

docked our boat on the shore, the first thing he did was call out my name, 'It is good that you have come to us, my brother Paphnutius; <you>[24] have been considered worthy to greet the holy ones.' And when he had greeted us, he took us joyfully inside his dwelling and said to us, 'Please offer a prayer, for you are holy men who have come to me today'. And when we had prayed we sat down and he brought a dish of water and we washed our feet. / [After we had washed our feet in the] /11b water, [he spoke], saying 'I am [not] worthy [of] this great gift, that you, my holy brothers, should come to [me] today'.

Paphnutius Hears From Isaac About Abba Aaron

28. After this, he set before us a table and we ate. And we gave thanks and sat down. I talked with him about his work and said to him, 'My father, you are very old'. The holy old man answered and said to me in a voice filled with joy, 'Forgive me, brother Paphnutius, my father, I am the least of all men, a sinner. Since you have asked about my work, I will tell <you>[25] the things that I have seen and heard when I was with my holy father Abba Aaron. Indeed, I sat as a disciple at his feet and I begged him to tell me the things he had seen and the things that had happened before his time. Now, my holy father Abba Aaron said, "I will tell you, my son, the things that I heard from the blessed Abba Macedonius / [the] bishop." ' /12a

Abba Aaron Tells Isaac the Story of Abba Macedonius

29. Now Macedonius said, '[When] I became governor and took over the rule of [Aswan?],

---

[24]Text: he.
[25]Text: me.

I came south and passed through the towns of this district and came into Philae. Because it was the Sabbath day, I looked for a place where I could participate in the eucharist, because I am an orthodox Christian and the people there worshiped idols; moreover, the few orthodox Christians among the population did not have freedom of speech on account of the multitude who worshiped idols. Therefore, I asked a man who was a Christian where I could find a church for the celebration of the eucharist. And he said, "Ah, my lord governor, we who live in this town are badly mistreated by those who worship idols. In spite of this, certain clergy who live in the town of Aswan regularly come to us and celebrate the eucharist for us on the Sabbath and the Lord's Day."

30. 'I, Macedonius, kept these things in my heart. And when I came to the city of Alexandria to pay my respects to the military governor, I sought out Abba Ath[anasius, the Ar]chbishop of Alexandria / and I told him everything I had seen. The holy wise man and rightful patriarch said to me, "Are there any there who worship God?" And I said to him, "Yes, my father; indeed, there was a Christian who told me that clergy from the city of Aswan go there and celebrate the eucharist for \<them\>[26] on the Sabbath and on the Lord's Day. Now then, my lord and father, find someone who is worthy to minister in this necessary work, ordain him bishop, and send him south with me." The holy archbishop answered and said to me, "Because you have taken this important matter on yourself, who is wiser than you or who can compare with you in understanding? You shall be the shepherd for the sheep in that place." And I said to him, "Forgive me, my holy father, I am

---

[26]Text: us.

not worthy to undertake something of [this] sort."
But he persuaded me / with his gracious words   /13a
[and ordained] me.

The Story of Macedonius and the Temple at Philae

31. 'Now when I came south, my brother Aaron, [I] distributed to those who [live] here everything I no longer had need of. I did not act with the authority of a bishop but I would walk as one who was the least among them. Now I saw them going into their temples and worshiping a certain bird that they call "the falcon"[27] inside some kind of mechanical device. Now it happened that after some days I came into [the courtyard of the temple]. The priest had left the city on business, [and] his two sons were performing his duties: they would take turns offering sacrifice to the idol. Now I, Macedonius, went up to them and using deceit spoke with them. I said, "I would like to offer a sacrifice to God today." And they said [to me], "Come and offer it." One of them went inside and ordered that wood be laid on the altar and a fire kindled beneath it, and the two sons of the priest watched over the wood until it burned down to the coals.' / [. . . Meanwhile] the bishop Abba Macedonius   /13b
went to where the mechanical device was. He removed the falcon, chopped off its head, and threw it upon the roaring fire. He left the temple and went away.[28]

32. Now when the sons of the priest saw [what] had happened, they tore their clothes. And the older one said to the younger, 'What are we going

---

[27]Coptic *bēc* (ⲃⲏϭ). Crum, *Coptic Dictionary*, 48B, lists a number of grecocoptic names in which the word occurs. Crum lists other instances where the falcon is mentioned in a religious context.

[28]For examples of Shenoute's destruction of idols, see Besa's *Life of Shenoute* 83–4 and 125–7.

to do? There's no way out of this for us. If the people of the city hear about it they'll stone us because we've been negligent and let their god be burned. But even supposing that we're able to save ourselves from them, we won't be able to escape our father—he loves the divine falcon more than us! Now then, my brother, we had better run for our lives to a place in the desert. Perhaps then we can escape him.'

33. And so the two brothers left the city that day. No one knew that God was watching over them, because they had been set aside as part of God's good plan. They crossed the Nile and came east, and they saw the mountain in the further /14a desert / and said, 'It is better for us to die here and have wild beasts devour our flesh than be stoned by the people of the city'.

34. Now it happened that when their father returned he went first to the temple to worship the idol (as was his habit) before he went home. When he went inside he did not find his sons. He went on into the sanctuary, but still did not find them. Next he turned to the mechanical device which held the falcon but did not find it, and so left, at a loss, saying, 'What can have happened? I can not find my sons, or even the divine falcon.'

35. A certain old woman, who lived close by the temple, heard him and called to him, saying, 'Come to me, blessed priest, and I will tell you what I saw today. I saw that law-breaking monk who has been leading some of the people of this city into error. He went into the temple with your sons—and, what is more, it was he who corrupted their minds! They took the divine [fal- /14b con] and fled!' Now the priest, / when he heard these words from the old woman, ran and looked throughout the city for his sons, saying, 'Not only will I kill my sons, but if I find that monk I'll kill him, too.'

36. Now a certain man, a believer, when he heard the old woman talking with the priest, went to the holy bishop and said to him, 'My noble father, listen to what this accursed temple priest said about you! He said, "If I find him, I will kill him." Now then, my holy father, rise and get yourself to a quiet place for a few days until this thing passes.' The bishop said to that man, 'Why, my noble son? I have heard from the blessed mouth of our God and Saviour, our Lord Jesus Christ: *Do not fear those who kill your bodies, but cannot kill your souls'*. That man said to the bishop, 'But he also said, *If they persecute you in this city, flee to another'*. The bishop said, 'Who told him that I went into the temple?' And he said to him, 'I heard an old woman who lives near the temple tell him'. The bishop said harshly, 'May her tongue become like iron and not wag again until the gift of God is revealed!' And it happened just as he said, just as the Apostle Peter said to Simon, *You shall be blind and not see the sun again*. When the holy bishop had said these words, the man removed himself from his presence.

Cf. Mt 10:28
Mt 10:23

Ac 13:11

The Vision of Abba Macedonius Regarding the Priest's Sons

37. The holy man rose and went north to the place called 'the valley'. He remained there and entreated God through fasting and frequent night vigils, saying, 'Lord God, turn the man's heart to repentance this night'. [Immediately] he saw a vision, as if [a man] were standing, and the two sons / were kneeling before him, one on his right and one on his left. A man of light came and stood over them. He placed a crown on the head of the one to the right, who was the elder, and another crown on the head of the one to the left. And he put a staff with a key tied to it in the hand of the one to the right, and another staff which had

/ 15b

another key tied to it in the hand of the one to the left. Then he ascended to heaven and <they> watched him with amazement.

38. The holy bishop Abba Macedonius rose in the morning and said, 'What was this vision that I saw? Are sons to be born to me after I have foresworn marriage?' It is too late for this! But your will be done, my Lord Jesus Christ.' Now, while the bishop was considering these things, a voice called out to him, saying, 'How long are you going to neglect the sheep which have been entrusted to you? Get up, and go to them, and /16a you will find [chosen] vessels / in that place.'

39. He rose and journeyed as he had been told. And when he had gone into the mountains a distance of about three miles he looked to his right and discovered the two sons lying under an overhang, half dead from hunger and thirst because they had neither eaten bread nor drunk water for six days. When the bishop saw them, he remembered the vision that he had seen, and he said, 'These are the two sons who were shown to me in the vision and these are also the ones about whom I was told, "Go, and you will find chosen vessels."'

Macedonius Tells the Story of Mark and Isaiah

40. Macedonius said: I walked toward them. When they saw me their spirits revived and they got up and prostrated themselves at my feet and kissed them. I myself helped them to their feet. And when I saw how weak they were from hunger and thirst, I stayed there with them. Now the /16b older one made a sign to the younger one / and said, 'Say something', while the younger one made a sign to the older one and said, 'You say something'. The older one replied, 'In very truth, [my] father, when I saw you I felt as though I had

eaten, although from the [day] we left the city we have neither eaten nor drunk nor have I seen anyone but you. And this is our sixth day. For it happened that last night—now I was not asleep, and my eyes were open—a man of light appeared, with a book in his hand, and he was wearing a splendid robe draped over his shoulder. He stood over me and made me get up. Now, when I stood up he dressed me in a tunic and fastened it with a shoulder-strap. When I had worn it a short time, he took it off me and gave it to my younger brother, and again fastened it with a shoulder-strap. When he too had worn it a short time, the man took it off him and gave it back to me. I looked on my right and / I saw you, my holy /17a father. That man of light took hold of me with his hand of light and drew me to his breast, and then he took my brother and drew him to his breast. Then suddenly he disappeared and I no longer saw him. Now then, my father, since we have been considered worthy to have you come to us, we are in your hands, soul and body, for indeed you were the reason we fled the city and came here.'

41. Now it happened that when the bishop heard these words he remembered what the Apostle said: *The spirit of the prophets shall come upon you.* Cf. Ac 2:17 He said to them, 'Rise, my sons, let us go, because God has determined that we should live together'. They rose and came down the mountain together and went to the place where the holy bishop lived, and the three of them lived together.

42. The bishop [said], / 'I will not eat with /17b them because they have not been baptized'. So he rose and filled a basin with water, as was his custom. He prayed over them according to the canons and said to them, 'What are your names?' The elder said, 'It is hard to say them in front of you, because the names we are called by are the names of gods', and they told them to the bishop. He said, 'You shall no longer be called by

these names'. And he gave a name to the elder one when he baptized him; he called him Mark. And the younger one he called Isaiah.

43. When he had baptized them, he administered the eucharist to them. Afterwards he set a table for them so they could eat. Now it happened that after they were with him a few days they were observing his manner of prayer and way of life and monastic routine,[29] for they knew no prayers except those they learned while living with the holy one. Mark said, 'My holy / father, we want you to shave the hair from our heads so we can serve you'. And he shaved their heads, and they obeyed him in everything. Now, it happened that after a few days the holy bishop remembered the vision which he had seen concerning the two sons, and he said, 'Truly, these are the two sons I saw, one on my right and one on my left'. And he took Mark first, and made him a priest, and Isaiah his brother he made a deacon.

/18a

The Story of Abba Macedonius and the Camels[29a]

44. Now it happened that as the bishop was sitting in his dwelling reading the holy gospels (Mark, too, was sitting there, by the door), certain Nubians who dwelled in that place came with their camels.[29b] One of the strong camels had knocked down a weak one and broken its leg.

---

[29]Gr.: *katastasis*.

[29a]Early in this century the holy woman (*sheikeh*) Sulūh solved a different problem regarding a camel: 'On one occasion, when a number of men and women had come to consult her, one of the former asked her what had become of his most valuable camel, which he had lost. The *sheikeh* at once told him the exact hour in which this loss had occurred, and informed him that one of his sons had stolen it and had sold it to a man in another village in the same province. She then told him the name of the man who had bought it, and said that if he went to the house of the purchaser he would be able to recover his loss promptly'. He did. See Blackman, p. 247.

[29b]Philae and Aswan lay on the border between Egypt and Nubia. On the

When the Nubians saw what had happened, they began to fight among themselves. The owner of the camel whose leg had been broken / said to the owner of the other one, 'I am going to take your camel to replace my own', and a great argument arose between the two of them. When Mark the priest saw them fighting with each other, he went and told the bishop. He decided not to go down to them, but when he came to the place in the lectionary where it is written, *Blessed are the peacemakers, for they shall be called children of God*, immediately he tied up the book and went down to them. /18b

Mt. 5:9

45. Now when the Nubians saw him, the one who had suffered the loss ran to him and said, 'Come and sit down, my father, and hear our case'. So the bishop sat down. The Nubian said to him, 'I tied up my camel, but my friend, he did not tie his. His camel came and knocked mine to the ground and broke its leg.' When this one had finished speaking, the other one said, '[It's not true,] / I did tie up my camel, but he broke loose, and I didn't know it.' /19a

46. The bishop had been sitting quietly until they finished all they had to say. Then the holy bishop said to them, 'Was there any other argument between you before today, or is this matter of the camel all there is?' One of them said, 'I will tell you the truth, my holy father. Look, we've traveled together for thirty years and we haven't fought with each other even a single day.' The holy bishop said, 'Bring me the camel whose leg is broken', and they brought it to him. It was true, the leg bone was broken and was being held together only by the hide, and the camel was walking with great difficulty, dragging its leg. When the holy bishop saw the animal [. . .].[30]

Nubians, see 'Aswan and Philae' above, pp. 54–69; for a detailed discussion, see William Y. Adams, *Nubia: Corridor to Africa* (Princeton, 1977).

[30] Two lines of the text here are very uncertain.

/19b He said to [his] younger [companion], / that is, Isaiah the deacon, 'Go and bring me a little water in a dish,' and he went and got it for him. He said, 'Sprinkle some on its leg, saying, "In the name of the Father and of the [Son and of the][31] Holy Spirit"'. And Isaiah made the sign of the cross over the camel as the bishop had told him, and its leg was healed as though it had never been broken at all.

47. When the Nubians saw what had happened, they were amazed, for they did not know God. Certain men, inhabitants of Philae, were passing by. When they saw what had happened, they glorified God and went to their town and spread the fame of the holy bishop concerning what they had seen. And they told the high priest of the temple (that is, the priest about whom we have spoken earlier) about his two sons, and that through the younger one the miracle had taken place.

Abba Macedonius and the Temple Priest

48. Now when the priest heard this, he hurriedly left [the temple] / and went to where the bishop and his sons were. Now the bishop had been told by the Spirit that the priest was drawing near his dwelling. He immediately rose and went outside and said to him, 'Aristos, what do you gain by leading astray this multitude and causing them to lose their souls?' And immediately the priest prostrated himself at his feet and kissed them again and again, saying, 'Forgive me, my lord father'. And the bishop took him by the hands and raised him up and took him inside his dwelling.

49. Now it happened that when the priest saw his elder son, Mark, he went up to greet him,

---

[31]Omitted from the text.

but Mark would not permit him, and said, 'You are not yet worthy of holy baptism'. When his father saw this he was amazed and said to him, 'Are you not [my] son?' And he said to him, '[Indeed] I am no son of yours. This very day I have got a good father.' / His father said, 'Tell me how I should live.' His son Mark said to him, 'Father, look, it is the bishop who will tell you how to live'. And the bishop began to speak to him from the holy Scripture and instructed him in the ordinance of baptism and the orthodox faith. And when the priest had heard these things, he said to the bishop, 'I am indeed blessed, my holy father, to have been considered worthy to hear these sweet words from your holy mouth. I beg you now, my holy father, to administer holy baptism to me as you did to my sons.' /20b

50. Now when the bishop saw that the fear of God was moving him and that his heart was set firmly on God, he said, 'I will not baptize you here, but rise and go to the city and attend to the affairs [of your] house and build a church.' / Now when the bishop had been instructing them a long time in the catechism, they said, 'Do not [delay]. Perform the rite of baptism.'[32] He consented, and added, 'Bring [me] oil', and Mark brought it. The bishop took [it] and prayed over [the water] and the oil according to the canons of the holy fathers the apostles, and he said to Mark the priest, 'Proclaim in the church "Whoever wishes the Lord, let him come to me."' And they came to him in a body with joy and gladness and he baptized them. He did the priest first. He baptized him and called his name 'Jacob'. /21a

51. Afterwards, he baptized the entire population of the city, men and women and little children. There was not a single person left who

---

[32]Literally: the rite of water.

/21b was not baptized that day. When the bishop finished the baptisms, he went into the church. He spoke, and summoned the man whom he wished to ordain priest [. . .] / '[. . .] our Lord Jesus'. [Now, the priest rose] and he went as the bishop had commanded him. He put his house in order [and gave] away everything he owned. He filled a vessel with water and washed himself [and] he arrayed himself in fine linen clothing. The priest sent [a message] to the bishop, saying, 'I have arranged everything as you ordered me. Rise, and come to the city.' And the bishop rose, he and his followers, and went.

52. When the people of the city heard about this, they rejoiced together, from the youngest to the oldest.[33] They came and took the bishop to the house of the priest and set him on a throne. And when he had sat down, a multitude gathered around him. He instructed them in the faith by means of the words of God [and taught] them about the ordinance of holy baptism and to love one another in the love that knows no hypocrisy. /22a [He saw Isaiah and called] / [to] him. He told him to hide himself so he would not be pursued on account of the priest. He ordained him deacon, then said to them, 'Where are your eucharistic vessels?' They said to him, 'They are hidden away'. And he ordered that they bring them quickly, and they rose and went immediately and quickly returned with them on their shoulders. And the bishop ordered them to set down the vessels in their midst. He said to Mark the priest, 'Strike the boards together to gather the multitude to the church,' and he did as he had been told, and the entire multitude gathered together. The bishop said to Jacob, 'See that good wine and bread are provided so I can celebrate the eucharist for [the multitude].'

---

[33]Or: from the least to the greatest.

Abba Macedonius Heals the Old Woman[33a]

53. Then he remembered [what the Gospel says: *If you] forgive [people their sins, you will also be forgiven by] / your heavenly father.* He told them to bring the old woman to him on a stretcher because she could not walk. They brought her and set her down before the bishop. The bishop said to her, 'Do you believe, old woman, that there is a God?' And she moved her head as if to say 'Yes'. (Now she was unable to speak because her mouth had been shut by the judgement that the bishop had passed on her.) The bishop Abba Macedonius rose and walked over to the stretcher and placed his finger in her mouth. Immediately the bonds holding her tongue were loosened and she was able to speak normally. She began to praise God. Now when the multitude saw what had happened, they gave a loud shout, saying, 'One is the God of the holy man Abba Macedonius the bishop [...] God [....' and the bishop] baptized [... the old woman. When] / he had administered the eucharist to the multitude, he went to the church and sat down with them there for a week. He ordained some of them priests and some deacons, and taught them the rules and canons of the Church. And after the seventh day he went home.

/22b
Cf. Mt 6:14

/23a

The Death of Abba Macedonius

54. Now it happened that after some days, his body was causing him difficulties, for he was very old. He called Mark the priest and Isaiah the deacon and said to them, 'Look now, the days of my stay here are drawing to a close. Now you, my son Mark, after I have completed my life, God

---

[33a]The old woman of paragraphs 35–36.

/23b will set you in my place. Sit on my throne, [my] son, and take good care of God's flock as I have entrusted it to you [. . .] from him [. . . .]' / He became sick, and the illness became more difficult for him. And he got worse and worse until the seventh of Mekhir.[34] He called his disciples and gave them orders about all their duties. And on the morning of the eighth of Mekhir, the holy bishop Abba Macedonius went to his rest at a good old age. When the people of his city heard about his death, they came to where he was and mourned him greatly on account of their deep love for him. And they prepared his body for burial in a manner befitting his rank, and they buried him outside his house.

Mark Succeeds Macedonius as Bishop

55. Now it happened that after the city had gone without a bishop for some time, all the people gathered together and said to one another, 'How long are we going to ignore this great duty incumbent upon us and not seek out a shepherd /24a to [watch over the flock of Christ?'] / [. . .] each deacon. They spent three days together talking with each other in this way without deciding anything. Now the chief priest of the church rose and stood in their midst and said, 'If you will listen to me, I have something to say which is worth your doing.' The majority of the people said to him, 'Tell us what it is and if it is suitable, we will do it.' And he said to them, 'Let us choose some men from among us, that is to say, men like Stephen and his companions, and let us cast lots. Cf. Acts We will take the one upon whom the lot falls 1:21–26, 6:3 and ordain him bishop'.

---

[34] 14 February.

56. Now it happened that when the priest had finished speaking, the archdeacon replied in turn and said, 'There is something I would like to say'. [And the people said,] 'Tell [us what you have to say.' He said, 'Who are these young men Mark and Isaiah?'] / They said, 'They are his sons'. The /24b archdeacon said, 'Look, they are now his heirs, and you have not considered them.' And when he said this, they remembered Mark and Isaiah. All the people responded, 'What the archdeacon has said is what will be.' And immediately they sent and brought them to the place where they were. They sat in the church and told Mark the priest what the archdeacon had said. But he said to them, 'Forgive me, my fathers. I am not worthy of a such a thing. Choose someone else who will care for the flock of Christ.' But all the people loved Mark because of his understanding and wisdom because he had been well instructed by his father, the bishop Abba Macedonius. So they took him by force and they wrote to the [holy] archbishop [Abba Athanasi]us concerning him. [And they took him] and [they boarded a ship with him and] / they sailed with him to /25a Alexandria.

The Story of Mark in Alexandria

57. Now when we entered the city, we sought out the patriarch but did not find him that day in the church because he was a holy man and dearly loved solitude. When some God-fearing[35] folk told us that he had withdrawn to the quiet of a small monastery on the west side of the city, we asked one of them to take us to him, for we did not know the place. When we arrived at the place where he was, a deacon came out and we spoke

---

[35]The text has 'fearing', here and *passim*. The sense is clearly 'God-fearing'.

to him about the matter we had come about. We went inside and told the archbishop and he had us shown in. We prostrated ourselves upon the ground and did homage at his holy feet.[36]

58. Now the holy archbishop Abba Athanasius had been informed by the Spirit [concerning the matter of our journey some] days [before we
/25b arrived. . . .] / Saint Athanasius replied and said to Mark, 'Have you forgotten, my son, when you were vested with the tunic and it was secured with the shoulder strap? This is the day that has been appointed for you, my faithful priest!' Mark was amazed at what he said to him, for he remembered the vision but had in fact talked with no one about it except Abba Macedonius the bishop and his brother Isaiah. And Mark said, 'You are truly a holy man of God, my blessed lord and father!' The archbishop said, 'You are much more holy than I, for you sat as a disciple at the feet of a bishop and holy man who was indeed holy'. Now when he had said these things, he ordered the deacon to take us to a place where we could be alone and he ordered [. . . .]

59. When it was morning [the archbishop had
/26a us shown in.] / Some members of the upper class from the western part of the city also came, wishing to receive a blessing from him. The deacon came in and told <him> about <them>.[37] He said, 'I am not free'. The deacon said to one of them, 'Please trouble yourselves and withdraw until tomorrow morning, for we have with us some brethren who have come on behalf of the people from the south'. When they heard this they

---

[36]Prostration and the kissing of feet as a sign of veneration for holiness was a common practice at this time, and occurs often in this text. See the *Life of Pachomius* 89 (Veilleux, p. 120). On the holiness of Athanasius and the esteem in which he was held by the monks, see the *Life of Pachomius* 201–2 (Veilleux, pp. 251–2). A letter from Athanasius to Horsiesos signals the end of the Bohairic and first Greek *Life*. See the *Life* 210 (p. 264).

[37]The text has 'them' and 'him'.

departed, saying, 'Pray for us, and we will go and pray in the monastery of Abba Menas, and we will return to you'.

60. Now we gave the document to the archbishop, and when he read it he rejoiced greatly and said to us, 'I rejoice greatly over the lost sheep in your city whom God, the lover of humanity, has turned to repentance'. He further told <us>[38] about the canons of the Church and said, 'What is your understanding of these things?' We [told him] according to what our father Abba Macedonius [had told] us. When the holy archbishop heard [what we said,] / [he said, 'Abba Macedonius laid the foundation and] we have built upon it. Truly, my children, not only did your holy father lay the foundation <and> build until he completed the foundation, he finished the foundation and the building and put the cornice piece upon it. To you yourselves now belongs the responsibility to do the things he commanded you.' /26b

61. When the archbishop had finished speaking with us, Mark the priest said, 'There is one thing which is a stumbling-block for me, and I would like to speak to you about it, my holy father.' The archbishop said, 'Go ahead'. Mark said, 'To the east of us and to the southwest of our city there are pagans[39] called the Nubians. They are very poor and they regularly call to us, "Give us bread". I am moved to say "No" to them because they are pagans [and do not worship] God.'

Archbishop Athanasius Teaches Mark About Love

62. [The archbishop said to him: 'Have you not heard the Lord say, *Seek, and you will* / *find; knock, and it will be opened to you?* Have you not /27a Mt 7:7

---

[38]Text: them.
[39]Gr: *ethnos*. See note 40.

heard the Apostle say, *Is God the God of the Jews only? Is he not the God of the other nations*[40] *also? Yes, he is the God of the other nations, because God is one.* He said to Abraham, *Behold, I have made you the father of many nations.* And again he spoke to Cornelius in the Acts (for he was a gentile).[41] Because God is one, God sent them Peter, the great apostle. He baptized Cornelius, and God taught Peter in a vision not to regard any person as impure or unclean.

Cf.
Rm 3:29–30
Cf. Gen 17:4

Cf. Ac 10:9–28

63. 'Mark, my son, how many citations do you need from the holy Scriptures in order to be convinced?' Mark said, 'I have sought, and I have [found. I have knocked, and it has been opened to me'. . . . (Mt 7:7–8)] / The archbishop said to him: 'Can it be that you have been ignorant of these things before now? Have you not read in the Gospels what our Saviour said to the Canaanite woman? He said, "It is not good to take the children's bread and throw it to the dogs". And she responded, saying, "Yes, lord, but the dogs also eat the crumbs that fall from their masters' table". Observe how our Saviour commended her answer. He said to her, *"Woman, great is your faith. May it be done for you as you desire."* And her daughter was healed from that time on because of what she had said'.

/27b

Mt 15:26–28

The Parable of the Two Monks Concerning Prayer

64. The archbishop also said: 'I will tell you another parable which I heard from our fathers the monks who lived in [. . . .There was a dispute about praying, whether it should be done privately or in the open. One brother said about another,] / "His work is not good. That which he

/28a

---

[40]Gr: *ethnos*, and below.
[41]Cf. Acts 10: 24–28. 'Gentile': *ethnos*.

does he does not do secretly. Indeed, James said in his catholic letters: / *The one who says, 'I am a worshiper' and does not bridle his tongue but deceives his heart, this person's worship is vain'* ". But another said, "His work is good. The holy psalmist David says, *I will offer my prayer before every one who fears the Lord.* Moreover, the Apostle says, *Pray without ceasing.* Indeed, there are many more places in the scriptures about prayer."

/sic

Js 1:26

Ps 22:25
1 Th 5:17

65. 'In reply, that first brother said, "Our Saviour told us, *You, when you are going to pray, go into your room and shut the door behind you and pray to your Father who is in secret, and your Father who sees you in secret will reward you*". The other brother said in return, "Here again, I for my part do not accept what you're saying". The first brother said to him, "Let's ask Abba Phou-p-koht, and he'll tell us the interpretation of that which we seek." [. . .] one another [. . .] / [. . .] (Now, the brethren had given him the name Phou-p-koht because he was not satisfied with anyone's way of life.)⁴²

Mt 6:6

/28b

66. 'The two brothers rose and went to him and called into his cell according to the rule of the brothers. He came out and took them into his place. They prayed and sat down together, and he said to them, "It is good that you have come". The brothers said to him, "Forgive us, our holy father". One of them signaled to the other to speak. The one who had found fault with the brother because he made a public display of his ascetic practices responded and told him about the argument between them. The old man answered, "Forgive me, brothers. Arguments over scripture only wear one out, for as soon as it is contained in one place it breaks out in another.

---

⁴²Coptic ⲫⲟⲥⲡⲕⲱϩⲧ, 'Casting Fire'. Crum, 134A, s.v. ⲕⲱϩⲧ, suggests that Phou-p-kōht might be a nickname and notes that the name appears in an Abydos graffito. Cf. Mk 3:17, where Jesus names the sons of Zebedee 'Boanerges', 'Sons of Thunder'.

But I will tell you a story about the things of this world. It happened one year that the Nile did not rise and flood all our fields with water, but only a few. Now there were two men in one house and one of them said, 'I will go out to /29a the field and sow a little seed / so we do not die of hunger and [perish].' The other one said, 'I myself will not go because there is not enough water to water all our fields.' Now, the one who had spoken first to his friend went and sowed a little wheat and a little barley and some lentils and a few beans and other kinds of seeds. Now the famine was widespread in the land. Now then, my brothers, which of these two will live: the one who sowed a little seed or the one who sowed nothing at all?"

67. 'The one who had caused the argument answered, "The one who sowed a little seed". The holy man said to him, "You have judged rightly, my son, for indeed the one who carries out fully a little commandment will live rather than the one who does nothing at all."[43] Immediately that brother, when he heard the rebuke, threw himself at the feet of the one he had quarreled with and said, "Forgive me, [my brother. . . ." And so he /29b received forgiveness] from him. / [. . .] the two.

68. 'Now then, my son Mark, I have told you these things on account of the pagans you told me about. It is better for you to force yourself to do something for love's sake, than to be forced without love in your heart, for *love covers a multitude* 1 P 4:8 *of sins*. As regards these pagans, they will come to believe in God after awhile, and therefore I have said all these things to you. I find you to be like a kernel of seed in its shell, as Isaiah says, *Do not destroy the one who has the Lord's blessing* Cf. Is 42:3; 65:8 *in him*'.

---

[43]For a parallel to this folk wisdom, see Thomas Merton, *The Wisdom of the Desert* (New York, 1960) p. 51 (Saying LXXVI).

The Consecration of Mark as Bishop

69. Now it happened that when the holy archbishop Abba Athanasius had said these things, he said to the deacon, 'Prepare the offering, for we will consecrate the bishop'. And so he rose and took Mark by the hand and led him into the church (the whole crowd was accompanying him) and he laid hands on him. He came out and went to [the] place where he lived and he said to [his] deacon, ['Prepare a table,] / so we can eat bread with each other.' And so we were considered worthy to receive the blessing of his holy Fatherhood. We spent three days with him according to custom and on the fourth day he gave us the episcopal license and dismissed us.[44] When we had gone out the door he sent his deacon to Abba Mark the bishop and he took him to him. And the archbishop said to him, 'When you go south to your city, lay hands upon your brother, first ordaining him deacon and afterwards priest.[45] He too has been appointed to the stewardship, for the tunic was also put on him and fastened with the shoulder strap. Now, as regards yourself, as you came under the protection of your father, so too shall your brother come under your protection. For this reason: after you have finished your days, it will be he who will sit in your place.' When Mark heard [these things from Abba Athanasius the holy] archbishop, [he departed] thus / and thus we left the holy archbishop.

/30a

/30b

---

[44]The Coptic for the term translated 'episcopal license' is *sustakē*, which is a corruption of the Greek *sustatikē*. Other corruptions of this same word occuring in the text are *sustalikē* and *sustadikē*. An *epistolē sustatikē* (the Coptic follows correct greek usage in using the adjective as a substantive) was a commendatory letter or letter of communion, especially 'carried by clergy or religious travelling to other dioceses or places where they were not known'. See Lampe, 1349B. See pars. 77 and 81.

[45]According to the narrative (¶ 43), Macedonius had already ordained Isaiah deacon. See ¶ 73.

Mark Returns South as Bishop

70. We went to Alexandria, setting sail in a small boat, and went to a place called Schissa.[46] There were a large number of boats tied up there. We visited all of them but did not find one headed for the city of Antinoe because in those districts they transport wheat. But God determined a piece of good fortune for us. After we had spent a few days there with the brothers and the bishop, we were saying, 'Why among all these ships haven't we found a ship going to our region?' The bishop said to <us>,[47] 'Be patient. God will send one to us in good time and we will go to our homes in peace.'

71. Now on the following evening there came into port a ship that belonged to the city of Aswan, a place not far from his city. Now the captain had brought his cargo north to the city /31a [. . . .] / Some noblemen had seized the boat and come aboard with their wives and their goods and all their baggage and their slaves and they came to Alexandria. Now when morning had come . . . the brothers who were traveling with the bishop looked and when they saw the ship they knew that it had arrived in port during the night. Immediately one of the brothers went and spoke with the captain of the ship, saying, 'Will you allow us to embark with you when you go south?' The captain said to him, 'Where are you from? I see that your speech is like ours.' And he said, 'We are citizens of Philae'. The captain said to him, 'What is your business here?' and 'Why have you come?' He began [to tell him that they had been waiting there] since [the ordination of the bishop. The captain rose and went to the /31b bishop and] / found him sitting at the door of the

---

[46]Schissa probably is Schedia, a grain port in the roman period, now called Kafr al-Dawar.
[47]Text: them.

church. He threw himself down and did homage at his feet. And he said, 'I am worthy of a great favor today, my holy father,' and he spoke and related to him how they had seized his ship. The bishop said to him, 'They will release it today, if it is God's will'.[48] And the captain ran off to the ship and related to the noblemen and his fellow sailors what had happened. And they too[49] ran to the church to receive a blessing from the bishop. He entreated the noblemen to release the ship to the poor and to take him south. And they said, 'It will be as you have commanded, our holy father.' And so [we left Alexandria] in a large ship [. . . .] / [With] Christ's help, the wind drove us with full force until we[50] arrived at his city.   /32a

72. And when they came south to their house they gave a great celebration for the bishop. And they presented him with some farm animals so they could seat him on them and take him to his city. Now when the people heard about the bishop, they all flocked out and with psalms and hymns they sang before him until they brought him into the church and seated him upon the throne.[51] And he showed them his episcopal license and the deacon took it and told the people that Mark and Isaiah were the heirs. The bishop read it to the people, and he celebrated the eucharist with his own hand and administered the sacrament to all of them, from the least to the greatest of them. He passed three days in the church instructing them in [the teachings

---

[48]There is a play on words in the Coptic: 'seized' is *keefe*; 'release' is *kaaf.*
[49]The text has 'And they too' twice.
[50]Text: they.
[51]For the chanting of psalms accompanying a bishop, see the *Life of Pachomius* 28 (Veilleux, p. 51). The bishop there is Athanasius. See Socrates, *Ecclesiastical History* 6.16, for the singing of hymns to accompany Chrysostom on his return from exile. See also below, ¶ 76. The singing of psalms was not, apparently, reserved for dignitaries; see *Historia Monachorum* 8.48 (Apollo); Russell, p. 77: 'We were seen and recognized from afar by the brethren, who had already heard about our arrival. . . .They came running to meet us, singing psalms. For this is what they generally do with all their visitors.'

/32b / of the Church and in the sacred Scriptures. . . .] / He performed many acts of charity and he kept all the commandments of his holy father Abba Macedonius the bishop.

73. Now after some days there was a great festival and all the people entreated him to come into the city and celebrate the eucharist with them. And while they were preparing for the eucharist, Mark called Isaiah his brother and he took him and ordained him a priest as the archbishop Abba Athanasius had commanded him. And so he celebrated the eucharist with the people; he blessed them and sent them away in peace.

The Death of Mark

74. Afterwards, when he had passed some days shepherding his people in the fear of God, his body lost its strength. He called his brother Isaiah and said to him, 'Listen to what I have to tell you. Since the holy archbishop Abba A[thanasius] said that the office of bishop was to be committed to you [after I had completed my days, you shall wear the tunic and shepherd the people of God'].
/33a / He lay down ill on the tenth of Tobe and so he went to his rest on the fourteenth of the same month.[52] And when the people were informed of his death, they came and kept watch over his body, and they all wept over him, saying, 'He was a good man'. And so they buried him beside the body of Abba Macedonius the bishop.

Isaiah Succeeds Mark as Bishop

75. Immediately they took hold of Isaiah the priest and that same day took him into the city,

---

[52] 22 January.

and they all persuaded him to let them appoint him shepherd over them in place of his brother Mark. And so they made a record of the votes cast in his favor and they gave it to certain God-loving brethren so they could take him to Alexandria and have hands laid on him. Immediately he went out to the ship, boarded it, and sailed north and, by the will of God, [they suffered no delay] and they reached [. . . Alexandria. Now before they arrived the archbishop was informed by the Spirit that they were coming.] / He said to them, 'He /33b is coming today. Now go to the church and keep watch there. When he comes he will go inside and receive Communion there today.'

76. Now while they were talking with the man, / the archbishop came and the people were /sic singing psalms before him. They went to him and threw themselves to the ground and paid homage to the archbishop. And he raised them up, saying, 'Rise, my children'. And they got up and received a blessing from him and gave him the list of votes cast in the election of the bishop. They accompanied him into the church and he sat down. Now when he had read the account of the voting he ordered the eucharist to be made ready. He rose and took Isaiah and led him into the innermost part of the church. He consecrated him bishop and Isaiah received Communion from his holy hands. [And when the archbishop had administered Communion] he sat down and had [Isaiah's appointment as bishop] written down. [The archbishop then blessed and dismissed us, and so we left the city.]

77. / We boarded ship and set sail and, by the /34a will of God, in a few days we came into port in the city of Aswan. The people heard about the arrival of the bishop and came out to meet him, and they sang before him and took him into the church and enthroned him. And Isaiah gave them his certification of appointment from the

archbishop and they read it. And in this way he dismissed them in peace. After spending three days in the church he came out and withdrew to his own house. And he did not go into the city except on the day of some great festival and also when the clergy came with all the clergy and the nobles of the people and they pleaded with him until he followed them.

The Death of Abba Isaiah

78. Now the blessed Isaiah was a good and benevolent man, and greatly loved. The rich [listened to his counsel and gave to the poor. Now when he had completed his life, he went to his rest. When the people heard,] / they came out and viewed his noble remains and they all mourned him, saying, 'He was a very good man'. When they had prepared his body for burial in a manner befitting his rank, they buried him beside his holy fellow-ministers, the blessed Abba Macedonius and Abba Mark, and afterwards each person withdrew to his own home.

/34b

Abba Pseleusias is Made Bishop

79. The city was some days without a bishop. Now there was a monk by the name of Pseleusias living on the island, and everyone who knew him testified to his works. This man our father Abba Aaron had made a monk when he was bishop. / Now God put it into the hearts of the people to seek him out, and the clergy and the people came out to the island and [they entreated him to shepherd the people of God. But Pseleusias refused, and said, 'I am not worthy of such a thing,] / for who am I? I am an ignorant man; I do not know my right hand from my left.' Now when they had

/sic

/35a

spent a considerable length of time entreating him and although he refused them, they seized him by force, put him on a boat, and took him to the city. They wrote out the list of votes that had been cast for him, and they sent with him certain other God-fearing brethren whom they commanded to watch over him until they got him to Alexandria and had him ordained.[53]

80. Now when they arrived at the harbor of Schissa, they boarded a small boat and set sail until they came to the city. When they came to the town gate, they found a brother and they asked him to tell them where the archbishop lived. Now the archbishop himself was sitting inside the gate and was conversing with two bishops, one from Athribis [and the other from. . . . And they told the holy archbishop that they had selected Abba Pseleusias as their bishop. But] / Abba Pseleusias /35b [told the archbishop, 'I am not worthy of such a thing'.] The archbishop said to him in a voice full of joy, 'My dear monk, day by day you have lived without cares or concerns. Today you will take on concerns very much like our own.'[54]

---

[53]The humble refusal of office is common in the monastic sources. See Chitty, *The Desert a City*, 87, and the *Life of Pachomius* 130 (Veilleux, p. 187). For other examples of monks ordained against their will, see Chadwick, *Cassian*, p. 14 (Archebius of Panephysis) and p. 30 (Cassian). See Cassian, *Institutes* 11.18 and 12.20 and *Conferences* 4.1.1. Cassian urged his monks to flee from bishops as from women. See also Henri Crouzel, *Origen* (Edinburgh, 1987) p. 19, for a list of others who fled ordination, including Jerome and Paulinus of Nola.

Palladius, *Lausiac History* 11 (Meyer, pp. 46–7), recounts a striking story: Ammonius, entreated by the citizens of a city to be their bishop, refuses, and so they appeal to Timothy, bishop of Alexandria (note the primacy of Alexandria here also). Ammonius still refuses and, while the embassy looks on, 'he took a pair of shears and cut off his left ear so he could not be ordained (see Lev 21: 17ff). When the bishop heard this, he said, "Let this law be kept by the Jews. If you bring me a man with his nose cut off, but worthy in other respects, I will ordain him."' But Ammonius, on hearing this, says, 'If you compel me, I will cut out my tongue.' They decided to leave him alone.

[54]One should compare this with the quite different speech given by Athanasius in the *Life of Pachomius* 28 (Veilleux, p. 52). Athanasius 'compared the refusal of responsibility to the concealment of the one talent in the Gospel'. See Chadwick, *Cassian*, p. 68. See Athanasius, Epistle 49.2, to Dracontius. The problem (from the

81. Now when the archbishop had said these things, he rose and took him into the church. He had them prepare the eucharist and the altar, and he prayed over him and ordained him as a reader; then he ordained him deacon, then he made him a priest and in similar fashion he consecrated him bishop. He then dismissed us, saying, 'Go in peace'. Now we left him, but forgot the letter of episcopal appointment. We went back to him and asked him for it, and he gave an order to his deacon and he took it from him /36a and he [wrote...] / 'Everything concerning the office of bishop which has fallen to me is beyond my ability or worth, saying, "I saw you being clothed in vestments and keys were being placed in your hands."'

Bishop Pseleusias Returns to the Island

82. Now it happened that after he had come south, the bishop went first to his place on the island, he and those who were with him. He stayed there because he was someone who greatly desired quiet contemplation. But when the people heard of this they were distressed. And they boarded some boats and came to the island, and when they had received a blessing from him they told him about the vacant see. The brethren who had gone with him told them that he had been consecrated. The people said to him, 'Why won't you come into the city, our father, as all the bishops have done?' And he said, 'Believe me, my children, I first wanted to see my own small home.' Now they brought him out and set him in a small boat, and they sang before him until they

---

bishops' point of view) did not abate: two centuries after Cassian, Pope Gregory the Great 'was still attacking monks who refused responsibility' (Chadwick, p. 68).

brought him into the church, and they seated him upon a throne according to custom. And in this way he celebrated the eucharist for all of them and dismissed them in peace. And the bishop Abba Pseleusias went into the church. / He spent sixteen days [teaching the] people by means of the word of God, and he [commanded] them to preserve their purity and love toward each other, and afterwards he returned home.[55]

/36b

Abba Pseleusias Goes to Alexandria: The Miracle of the Baptismal Font

83. Now it happened that after these things Abba Timothy went to his rest and Abba Theophilus sat on the episcopal throne.[56] And all the bishops went to Alexandria to pay their respects to him. Now the holy man Abba Pseleusias also went. And when they arrived in the city they found the archbishop in the church with all the clergy and people gathered together around him. It was the seventh day of the week,[57] the day on which they were accustomed to doing baptisms. Now when the font had been filled with water, the archbishop came in with the other bishops and they prayed over 'the Jordan'. But Abba Pseleusias stood off by the door of the baptistry, at a little distance away. He did not go inside because he considered himself unworthy.

84. Now the archbishop was informed about him by the Spirit. He ordered him to be brought in, and he said to him, 'Why did you not come

---

[55]Pseleusias, like James of Nisibis, is a monk made bishop. See Theodoret, *History* 1.7 (Price, p. 15): 'Although he exchanged that life on the hills and chose against his will to dwell in a city, he did not alter either his food or his clothing, but although there was a shift of place his way of life underwent no change.'

[56]That is, as archbishop of Alexandria. This event dates this part of the history to 384.

[57]Saturday, the Sabbath.

/37a / [into the baptistry] and pray with us?' [And he] said to the archbishop, 'Forgive me, my holy father, I am a humble man,' and he stretched out his hands and prayed together with them. Immediately the font began to boil like a bronze cauldron and became red-hot. When the archbishop and all the other bishops saw the miracle which had taken place, they glorified God and the holy bishop Abba Pseleusias because of his purity. And when the archbishop had finished the baptisms he administered Communion to them and dismissed them. The bishops remained with him that day, and the next day he sent them away so each one could go to his own city.

The Death of Abba Pseleusias

85. Now the holy man Abba Pseleusias for his part remained quietly in the place where he had first lived before he became bishop until the day when he completed his life. He lay down sick on the twentieth of Paone and subsequently went to his rest on the twenty-third of this same month.[58] And all the clergy and people came out and they /37b viewed his glorious body. / They buried him in his [own] glorious [resting] place.

III. THE LIFE OF ABBA AARON

86. Now then, my brother Paphnutius, since you <asked>[59] me for some information, you see, I have told you about the bishops who lived in Philae. According to what my father Abba Aaron told me personally, his parents paid money and bought him a commission in the army. And he

---

[58]30 June.
[59]Text: told.

received seven loaves of bread daily but he never ate any of them; instead, he gave them away in accordance with the commandment. His parents wanted to take a wife for him, but he refused. Instead, he remained a virgin from his birth until he completed his life.

Mt 6:29

Abba Aaron and the Lion

87. Now it happened one day that letters were sent to the imperial troops ordering their transfer to another city. And the order came to Abba Aaron to take the troops and go with them. Now when he left the city a lion met him on the road that evening and wished to seize him. And the righteous man said, 'When I remembered the words which the prophet David said, *The lion and the bear has your servant slain,* I raised my eyes / [to heaven] and said, "My Lord Jesus Christ, [if you] deliver this wild beast into my hands, I will give up my house and everything in it and all my possessions and I will become a stranger to my parents and to all my men and I will become a stranger to the things of this world, and I will clothe myself in the monastic habit for the sake of your holy name." '

1 Sam 17:36
/38a

88. And now the holy man Abba Aaron said, 'When I had said these words, I made ready the spear in my hand. I drove it through the lion and he died. And I did not return to the city right away but went to another town a three day march to my south. When I got there I sold my horse and my tunic with all its accouterments and all the things I had with me. I bought myself some clothes like the countryfolk wear, and with the rest I ministered to the poor in that place. Then I went to the monastic community of Scetis and there I put on the monastic habit. But I did not remain there because of my parents, for they were

searching for <me>,⁶⁰ and so I traveled south, little by little, until I came to this community.'

/38b Now these things which I have just told / you, my brother Paphnutius, [I heard] from my father Abba Aaron.

Abba Isaac Relates His Own Story to Paphnutius

89. When I asked him to tell me his own experiences after he renounced the world, after a while he added: 'If you will pray for me, I will tell you the things I have seen with my own eyes. Now it happened that when I was a child in my parents' house, my parents sent me to school so I could be taught to write. Now my teacher diligently instructed me every day until he had taught me to write the holy letters. When I had made sufficient progress in my learning, I was able to read the passage from the Gospel which says, *Whoever will not forsake father or mother*, and the rest

Mt 10:37 that follows, *and follow me, is not worthy of me*. I pondered this passage in my heart and I continued to meditate upon it with my whole heart.

Isaac Goes to See Abba Aaron

90. 'Now it happened that after some days I heard a report about our holy father Abba Aaron that he was living the monastic life in a place called "the valley" and was performing many cures for all those who were sick. I rose and went to where he was living. I sat by the door of his dwelling

/39a until the sun set, for that day was a holiday. / When evening had come and he had not come out, I rose and walked about three miles into the desert.⁶¹ After a while I looked down into the

---

⁶⁰Text: him.
⁶¹Or: mountain.

sand and I saw footprints headed around a corner in the rock. I followed them and found my holy father Abba Aaron, and hanging from his neck there was a rope to which was tied a large stone.

91. 'Now when I called out to him, "Bless me", he withdrew his neck from the rope and threw the stone to the ground, and put on his clothes. He gazed into my face and said to me, "Where are you going, my son, in this place?" And I said to him, "Forgive me, my father, for I am lost". He said to me, "Come, sit down, my son. Indeed, you are not lost; rather, you have found the good path." When I had seated myself beside him, I entreated him, "I want to ask if you will let me be a monk with you." He spoke to me with compassion, "Our Saviour says in the Gospels, *Come to me, everyone who is weary, and I will give you rest.* The monastic life has become / well-known, but this way of life is labor and suffering up to the very end."[62] I said to him, "My holy father, it is for this very thing that I have come here! If I am to complete my life in perfection, you must show me mercy." He said to me, "That which you seek is good, my son. Since you have put your hand to something which is good, who will be able to stop you, my son?"

Mt 11:28
/39b

Isaac Becomes a Monk

92. 'Now we rose and came out from the desert, and he took me to a priest to clothe me in the monastic habit. And when we called inside the priest's house he came outside and greeted us and took us inside his place. Right away my father told

---

[62]The Coptic has a play on words in this passage. 'To the very end' is *jokef ebol*, the same words translated 'to complete in perfection' in the next line. For a similar story, see the *Life of Pachomius* (Bohairic 10, First Greek Life 6; Veilleux, pp. 30 and 301).

him about me and immediately the priest shaved the hair from my head and clothed me in the monastic habit. We rose and went home. Now my holy father Aaron spent a week in helping me lay the foundations for doing work in the service of God. After a week he said to me, "Stay here while I go and visit this brother and then I will come back and see you." (Now he did not want /40a me to know that he wanted / to go keep his own monastic observances.) And I said to him, "Will you come back today?" And he said to me, "No, my dear brother. Give me until the Sabbath."

93. 'The first day on which he left me was the [?].[63] And he spent the first day and the second and the third and even the fourth and fifth away from me. Now as for me, demons were severely abusing me: "Why did your father leave and leave you all alone? Why didn't he take you so you too could be blessed by that brother?" Now when they continued to trouble me, I rose and set out into the desert to where I had found him the first time. I discovered him standing out in the sand (it was very hot, since it was the season when the Nile floods). There was a huge stone sitting on his head and his eyeballs were about to burst on account of the heat. He fell to the ground and gave himself up to die. I grabbed him and raised him up, weeping into his face, saying, "Why do you punish yourself so badly like this, /40b my holy father?" / And he said to me, "Why have you come here my son?" I said to him, "The Nubians have been tormenting me, and I've come to tell you."

94. 'He smiled and said, "Truly, they are invisible Nubians, my son." I entreated him, saying, "I beg you, your holy Paternity, why do you give yourself to such afflictions and ascetical practices?"

---

[63]The meaning of the Coptic *pouosh* (ⲡⲟⲩⲱϣ) is not clear here.

That very old man Abba Aaron answered, "I will not hide anything from you, my son, regarding your question. Indeed," he said, "when I remember the afflictions which my good Saviour endured for us until he redeemed our race from the captivity of the devil—he gave his body and blood for us—I say, 'Since God took it upon himself to suffer on our behalf, it is right that we too should have every kind of affliction until he has mercy on us on the day of reckoning' ". And when he had said these things, we rose and left and came home.

Cf. 1 P 2:12

Abba Aaron's Way of Life

95. 'Abba Aaron lived the monastic life in this manner. On the day he ate / he would drink no water, and the day he drank water he would not eat. Now it happened that one night when we were both sleeping at home, the demons took on fantastical shapes and were crying out in the valley below with the voices of roaring lions. When I heard them I was terrified and so I shook my father awake and said, "Lions are attacking us!" But he said to me, "Do not be afraid, my son, for it is written: *Through our God we shall do a great thing*, and again, *Let God arise, and let his enemies be scattered*". After he said these things, we rose and went to the upper room. The demons were crying out as before and some of them were saying, "Bring them here so we can kill them", while others were saying, "Let's kill them where they are." The holy one knew through the Spirit that they were demons and he said to me, "Let us give ourselves to prayer". And as soon as we had given ourselves to prayer, the demons fled through the valley.

/41a

Ps 60:12
Ps 68:1

96. 'Now I was amazed and said to the holy old man Abba Aaron, "Don't demons assume a number of forms?" / And he said, "You will see,

/41b

my son, that what you have accomplished is a small thing indeed. For a certain brother spoke to me, saying, 'It happened to me once that I was standing under a mountain ledge one summer's day. For six days I had neither eaten nor drunk nor sat down. A demon came, carrying a golden staff in his hand, and he said to me, "Be strong, athlete of Christ, and fight the good fight. For I have seen your sufferings, and I have been sent to comfort you."' Now that brother, when he perceived the wiles of the Devil, drew the sign of the cross on the ground and immediately the demon disappeared."

97. 'Now it happened that when the holy man Abba Aaron said these things to me, I threw myself down at his feet and I entreated him, saying, "Who was that brother?" And he said, "Rise, and I will tell you." And when I had gotten up he said to me, "See that you tell no one! I was this servant, and I was completely unworthy for this to have happened to me."

Abba Aaron and the Miracle of the Nubian's Son

98. 'Now it happened that on another day we were sitting with one another. A certain Nubian came out from the mountain with his son to drink /42a water from the river. / And when his young son put his hand into the river to scoop up some water to drink, a huge crocodile seized him and dragged him under and fled. Immediately his father threw himself to the ground and cried out and wept bitterly, for besides that son he had no other. Now as the man ran up the mountain crying out, he cut himself against the sharp edges of the rocks and severely injured himself. When I saw how heartbroken he was, I told my father. He got up and came to the door and gestured to the Nubian

with his hand to come to him. And when he had come, Abba Aaron saw the wounds on his body, and he wiped away the blood that had run over his body and took him and brought him inside his home. He brought him in by force and made him sit down.

99. 'Now when he had questioned him about what had happened (he could not understand what the Nubian was saying to him), my father said to me, "Rise, see if you can find anyone on the road. Call him. Perhaps you can find someone who knows how to speak with him. When I went out I found a man from Philae who was going to Aswan riding on a donkey. I called to him / and said to him, "Do you understand the language of the Nubians?" He said, "Yes". I took him to my father Abba Aaron. Now when that man saw the Nubian and the wounds all over his body, he was astonished and said to him, "How were you wounded?" and the Nubian told him what had happened. The holy man Abba Aaron took a piece of wood and gave it to him, saying, "Take it and throw it into the river where the crocodile seized your son." And he went and did as Abba Aaron had told him. /42b

100. 'Now it happened that when he threw the piece of wood into the water, a huge crocodile appeared and cast the little boy up on the shore— and he had not been injured in any way! And his father took him by the hand and brought him to the holy old man Abba Aaron. And when the Nubian saw this miracle, he shouted with joy and hugged Abba Aaron and kissed him. Now the interpreter went to Philae and did not go to Aswan that day; instead, he went about proclaiming the miracle that had taken place. And when the Nubian saw the miracle that had taken place, he went home glorifying / God and proclaiming what had happened. And all those who heard /43a

glorified God and the holy man Abba Aaron until this very day.

Abba Aaron and the Miracle of the Fisherman's Son

101. 'Now it happened that on another occasion one day when we were sitting at home, a fisherman came to us. His clothes were torn, his head was covered with dust, and he was weeping bitterly. I went up to him and said, "What happened to you?" And he said to me, "It happened that I and my small son, who was in the boat with me, were dragging in our net when he fell into the water and got tangled in the net and I could not pull up the net because of the very strong currents. When I remembered my lord, the holy father Abba Aaron, I rose and I have come to him to seek his mercy and favor, for this is my only son." And I got up and went and told my father. He got up and came down. The man prostrated himself at his feet and worshiped him, saying, "Help me! Ask Christ to be gracious to me and give me back my son, for I have no other."

/43b / 102. 'Now that glorious old man said to him, "Go, my son, in the name of the Lord. I believe that you will find your son sitting in the boat." And he said, "I believe, by God, that it will happen just as you have said." And he went to the boat and found his son just as Abba Aaron had told him. He asked his son, "What happened to you?" and he said, "It happened that when I got tangled up in the net and was about to lose my last breath, I looked and saw a man of light. He took me by the hand and freed me from the net, and brought me up into the boat. And suddenly I no longer saw him." And his father took him and brought him to the holy man Abba Aaron, and gave thanks to God and to the holy man Abba Aaron.

Abba Aaron and the Miracle of the Vineyard Worker

103. 'There was also a certain laborer who lived a little to the south of us and worked in a vineyard. Now it happened that when he had climbed up a date palm tree to gather dates, the belt holding him broke. He fell backwards to the ground and seemed to be dead. Now his son was sitting under the palm tree and when he saw what had happened, he wept bitterly. And when the men who were nearby / [heard] him crying out, they went to see what had happened. When they saw their friend lying on the ground as though dead, they said to his son, "Go to the holy man Abba Aaron, and get a small bowl of water from him in faith and throw it on your father. Maybe he will wake up." /44a

104. 'The young boy went weeping to the holy one. Now the holy one was sitting by the door because he had a fever and was exhausted. The young man threw himself down before him and told him what had happened. Now when the righteous and compassionate one heard what had happened, his heart was heavy and he said to me, "Bring me a little water, and let the young man take it and throw it on his father in the name of Christ. So I brought the water to him. He made the sign of the cross over it and gave it to the young man to take and throw it on his father. As soon as he threw it on him, he immediately got up. He came with his son and worshiped at the feet of the holy man Abba Aaron. The holy one raised him up, saying, "Worship God, for I am the least of God's servants." When he rose, his son told him what had happened, saying, / "When I threw the water [on] you, you trembled and then stood as though you'd just woken from sleep." And so they went away from him in peace. /44b

Abba Aaron and the Miracle of the Stillborn Baby

105. 'Now there was in Philae a woman who was about to give birth but her child withered inside her and died.[64] And when she remembered the miracles which God had worked through the holy man Abba Aaron, she cried out, saying, "God of the holy man Abba Aaron, hear me in the hour of my distress!" Immediately she gave birth to a small child, but he was dead. And her parents greatly mourned for the small child, but when the young woman saw her parents' heavy hearts, she said to them, "Why are you so heavy-hearted about the child?[65] Had I not asked the God of the holy man Abba Aaron, I too would have sunk into death."

106. 'Now when her parents heard this, they took money in their hands (for they were very wealthy) and went to the holy man Abba Aaron. (Now the Spirit told him, "They will be coming to you.")[66] He said to me, "Shut the door and do not allow anyone to see me today." When /45a / they arrived, they spent a long time knocking on the door and calling inside. And he looked out through a window and said to them, "Who are you looking for?" They answered, "We are looking for your Holiness." Then he said, "What do you need?" And they said, "We have come to meet your Holiness. Accept this small gift and pray that the child might live for his mother's sake. Indeed, his mother called upon your name when

---

[64]The Coptic for what is translated here as 'withered' is *joht*, literally 'failed, ceased'. There is a play on words here: 'child' in Coptic is *sherē*; 'miracle' in the following line is shperē.

[65]The word-play continues: the Coptic for 'small child' is *pshēre shēm*; 'young woman' is *tsheere shēm*.

[66]On the holy man being informed through God or the Spirit, of which we have several examples in this narrative, see the *Life of Pachomius* 107 (Veilleux, p. 158). In the *Histories* the holy archbishops of Alexandria also have such powers; see pars. 58 and 84.

she was about to give birth. Had she not done so, they would have both died."

107. 'Saint Abba Aaron said to them, "The Apostle has well said, *The root of all evil is the love of money.* And Peter rebuked Simon, saying, *May your silver and your gold go with you to perdition because you think that the gift of God is acquired by money.* For it was through the love of money that Gehazi was cursed with leprosy. Furthermore, our Lord said to the imperial officer, 'Go, your child lives,' and the officer had offered him neither gold nor silver. Now as for you, if you believe, the gift of Christ will be given to you." They answered, "We believe, our holy father, that Christ will fulfill everything you say to us." 1 Tm 6:10
Ac 8:20
2 Kgs 5:27
Lk 7:1–10

108. / 'And the father of the child / [took] a little earth from beside the door of Abba Aaron's home and tied it up in his neckerchief. And when they came into the house they found a large crowd of people gathered together and the man's wife and her child. The child's father uncovered the little bit of earth tied up in his neckerchief and sprinkled it upon the dead child. Immediately he moved his body and opened his eyes. Those who were sitting beside the mother were astounded and they glorified the God of the holy man Abba Aaron.[67] Now the people used to bring large numbers of the sick and diseased to Abba Aaron and he would heal them. He was like the apostles to whom God gave power over every kind of sickness. /45b /sic

Abba Aaron and the Rich Man and the Poor Man

109. 'Now on another occasion a man from the city of Aswan came to Abba Aaron one day. He

---

[67]There is another word play here: 'child' in Coptic is *pshēre*, while 'astounded' is *shpēre*.

continuously wept before him and said, "There is a certain rich man in my city whom I owe ten obeli, and I can not get the money to pay him. I have begged him, 'Be patient with me and I will repay you.' But he would not agree to this and has seized me for what I owe him. He wants to take from me my vineyard which I inherited from my parents and from which I make a small profit, enough for my poor children and me to live on.

/46a / I am paying him the interest I owe him. I beg you, your Holiness, to send a message to him to ease up on me, for someone from his household told me, 'He's going to press you for the principal and haul you into court so he can take away your vineyard.' But I believe that if you were to send a message he would not refuse to listen to you." As he said these things, he wept.

110. 'Now evening had come and the man rose to go on home, but Abba Aaron saw his distress and said to him, "Stay here until morning, for it is late now", and he stayed in the outer court. My father Aaron said to me, "Take a loaf of bread and some water and give them to him and say to him, 'Stay here until morning, and God will help you.'" And I did as he told me, but the man, because of his sadness, refused to taste anything. And I went and told my father and he came out to him and said to him, "Do not be disobedient, my son. Rise and eat a little bread and I believe /46b [that] God will help you." / And in this way he persuaded him. The man rose and ate.

111. 'Now the holy man Abba Aaron rose and went to the upper room. He spent the whole night petitioning God and praying on behalf of that man. When morning came, the man tried to return home but the holy man Abba Aaron said to him, "Stay here a little longer and you will go home with your mind at ease." And while these words were still in his mouth, the rich man came riding on a donkey which was being led, and two

other men were following him in order to guide him to the righteous one. His eyes were open but he could not see. He threw himself down at my father's feet and worshiped him. Abba Aaron took hold of him and raised him to his feet. Then the holy one said to him, "Have you not heard the law which says, *You shall not covet any of your neighbor's possessions: not his house or his field or his livestock or his vineyard or his olive trees.* [. . .] It [says] also, *[Woe to those who join] house / to house and field to field and take away their neighbors' possessions.* This word 'woe' makes it perfectly clear that severe punishments lie in store for whoever covets his neighbor's things, from the greatest person to the least. Again the Saviour cried out, *Blessed are the merciful, for to them shall mercy be shown.* Then again, *Mercy shall make a man triumph over judgement.*"   Ex 20:17; Dt 5:21 /47a Is 5:8; Mi 2:2   Mt 5:7, 6:14 Jm 2:13

112. ' "Be merciful in this world, my son, that mercy may be shown to you in the other world where you are going. It is good for you to have compassion on the poor so that the merciless misery and poverty of Nineveh not be yours,[68] because judgement is without mercy towards him who does not show mercy. Again, 'Mercy shall make a man triumph over judgement.' Have you not heard about Ahab and what happened to him when he coveted the vineyard of Naboth the Israelite"?   1 Kgs 21:13–19, 22:34–38

113. 'Now when the holy man Abba Aaron had said these words to the rich man, the latter answered, saying, "Have mercy on me, righteous and honorable one! Please ask Christ on my behalf

---

[68]In coptic literature, Nineve is the name given to 'Dives', the unnamed rich man in the parable told by Jesus about a beggar named Lazarus (see Lk 16:19–31). For a discussion of a coptic homily attributed to Saint Peter, bishop of Alexandria (d. 311), which includes an elaborated retelling of the Nineve and Lazarus parable, see Tim Vivian, *St. Peter of Alexandria: Bishop and Martyr* (Philadelphia, 1988) 59–62; for the homily itself, see Birger A. Pearson and Tim Vivian, *Two Coptic Homilies Attributed to St. Peter of Alexandria* (Rome: forthcoming).

/47b

that this darkness over my eyes cease, and I will never disobey you in anything." The holy one said to him, / "Do you believe that I am able to do this?" The rich man answered, "Oh yes, I do, my holy father! What is more, listen to me and I will relate to your Charity what happened to me. Now it happened that when the man about whom you have spoken with me had left yesterday, I went up to my house and went to bed. I woke up at night and sensed this great darkness over my eyes. And when morning came I said to my household, 'I cannot see today'. Now they said to me, 'Clearly this has happened to you through the holy man Abba Aaron. We saw the man with whom you were talking yesterday about money go to him.' As soon as I heard that he had gone to your Holiness, I knew that this had happened to me because of him. I myself have come to you because this I believe: that you have the power to heal me."

114. 'The holy man said to him, "If you show mercy to the poor man, Christ himself will heal you." The rich man called one of those who had come with him, and he took the loan agreement from him and gave it to the righteous man Abba Aaron. The holy man Abba Aaron said to him,

/48a "[If you give wages to the poor man] / in this world, God will give you your wages in the world to come." Then he made the sign of the cross over the rich man's eyes. Abba Aaron said to him, "Wash your face in faith". Now as soon as he had washed his face, he was able to see. Those who had accompanied him were amazed and glorified God.

115. 'The rich man rose and prostrated himself before the holy man Abba Aaron, giving thanks both to God and to Abba Aaron because he could see. The holy one gave the loan agreement to the poor man and commanded him, saying, "You too are to be merciful to your neighbor, as mercy has been shown to you. Do not ever say, 'I am a poor

man, I am not able to keep the commandment in the Gospel.' The Gospel will never accept from you any excuse you make, poor man. But even for something as small as a cup of cold water, God will reward you! Do not be like that worthless servant whose lord forgave a debt of many talents. He went and squeezed his fellow-servant for the little bit he owed him. No, be like the wise servant who doubled his talent". / The poor man answered, "Pray for me, my holy father, and I will keep everything which you require of me." And in this way both men profited, and they left Abba Aaron, glorifying God.

Mk 9:41
Mt 18:28
Mt 25:14–23
/48b

Abba Aaron Heals a Man's Gout

116. 'Now when the rich man went home he told his household everything that had happened to him. Now there was a man in his house whose feet had for a long time caused him great pain. When he heard the miracles which the holy one had done, he said, "How I wish I were worthy to meet him, so he would have mercy on my misery and I would be healed!" The man with the gout said to the rich man, "Didn't Abba Aaron touch some part of your body?" He said, "Yes, he did. He touched my hands. I had thrown myself at his feet and he raised me up by my hands and I worshiped him. The man with the gout said to <him>,[69] "Please come near me." Now when the rich man drew near to him, he took his hand and placed it upon his feet, saying, "I believe [that if the] hand [that touched] the holy man Abba Aaron [touches my feet, I too will be] / healed." And so the pain left his feet that very hour, and everyone who heard about it glorified the God of Abba Aaron.

/49a

---

[69]Text: me.

Abba Aaron and the Miracle of the Donkey

117. 'Now there was also in Philae a man who owned a donkey that he worked in the mill. When he was getting ready to go home, the donkey fell down right there at his feet and died. But he, because of his great faith in the righteous man, left the donkey lying there dead and ran to him and told him about it. Now the righteous one said to him, "He has not died, my son, but has fainted." He gave him a staff and said to him, "Go and strike him with it three times and he will stand up." And he took the staff and left and struck the donkey with it three times and it got up on its feet as it usually did. The man came to my father and said to him, "Thank you, my father, for the favor which God has shown me." Now my father admonished him not to tell anyone what had happened, saying, "Do not allow anyone to disbelieve our words. For indeed our Saviour said, *[Truly, truly, I say to you, whoever believes in me, the works which I do] / he shall do also, and he shall do things greater than these*."

/49b
Jn 14:12

Abba Aaron and the Miracle of the Vineyard

118. 'Now the holy man Abba Aaron would himself do a great deal of work with his hands, for he remembered what is written, *We worked with our hands by day and by night, so that we might not add to the toil of any of you*. Sometimes he made grave-clothes and sometimes he plaited rope. And he was never in a hurry to speak unless there was some great urgency. A man came to him one time and bought some cord from him for use in his vineyard. Now that vineyard's stock[70] was very

1 Th 2:9

---

[70]Coptic: čelma. Čelma ('jar') is probably a mistake for čelm̄ ('dry sticks'), the root stocks of the vines.

hard, but when he took the cord from Abba Aaron he got a very good harvest. And those who heard about it glorified God.

Abba Aaron and the Miracle of the Fish

119. 'On another occasion, some fishermen came to him, downhearted, and they entreated him, saying, "Please pray for us. We are being harassed by a certain nobleman about a large quantity of fish, which we have not been able to catch and deliver to him. We're afraid that he will hold us liable and sue us for damages beyond our ability [to pay."... Abba Aaron replied and said, "Have you not heard that the Lord said to] / Peter, *Cast your net on the right side of the boat, and you will catch something?* He did not say 'on the left side', but 'on the right side,' which means that when someone abandons himself to evil thoughts, that is to say, to things that are on the left, he does evil. When he does the things of the right hand, that is, things that are good, everything that he asks from God will come to him.

120. ' "To be sure, the Lord spoke this way to those on the left: *Depart from me, you accursed, into the everlasting fire that has been prepared for the devil and his angels.* But to those on his right hand he said, *Come to me, you blessed of my father.* And again he said, *Come to me, everyone who is weary and burdened, and I will give you rest.* And again, *You will inherit the kingdom that has been prepared for you from the foundation of the world.* Why? He said, *I was hungry and you fed me; thirsty, and you gave me something to drink. I was naked, and you clothed me; I was a stranger and you accepted me among <you>*.[71] *I was sick and you visited me; in prison, and you came*

/50a

Jn 21:6

Mt 25:41
Mt 25:34

Mt 11:28

Mt 25:34

---

[71]Text: us.

Mt 25:35–36
/50b

to see <me>.⁷² All this means that if you cast your net on the right side, / you yourselves shall catch many fish, according to your need."

121. 'And they said to him, "We swear by your salvation, our holy father, it is because of our poverty that we have not had the leisure to go to church on the Sabbath and on the Lord's day!" He said to them, "Have I said to you, 'You haven't been going to God's church'? If you ask him, he will have mercy on you, and he will not let you be in need of anything, for it is the duty of all Christians to go to the house of God first thing in the morning and pray to him to make ready the work of their hands."

122. 'And they prostrated themselves at his feet, saying, "Pray over us, our holy father, and we will obey all your words." And so he prayed over them and gave them a bowl of water, saying, "Sprinkle this over your nets, and you will catch something." Now they left in faith and they caught a large number of fish. They gave the nobleman as many as he wanted and they kept the rest for the needs of their household. And they came to the righteous man and they gave thanks to God and <to him for> his holy prayers [...]

/51a

/ immediately. Now there was also another man whose ship was in danger of sinking, and when he called upon God in the name of Abba Aaron, his ship was saved, with all its cargo.

Abba Aaron and the Miracle of the Man Blind in One Eye

123. 'Now it happened that one day two Nubians were walking together on their way to Aswan. One of them had only one eye. His friend said to him, "Come on, let's receive a blessing at the hands of this great man." The one-eyed man said, "He isn't a great man; if he really is, let

---

⁷²Text: him.

him open my eye," and while the words were still in his mouth, his eye—which had been blind—regained its sight, but his good eye became blind! When his friend saw what had happened, he was utterly amazed, and said to him, "Didn't I tell you that he is a very great man?" The one-eyed man said, "It's no great loss, for one eye has been shut while the other has been opened. However, let's go to him; perhaps he'll give light to the other eye." So the two of them came to the holy man Abba Aaron. My father said to the Nubian, who was not a believer, "Since you think it's no great loss, why are you here?" Immediately he became very [fearful] and worshiped him, saying, "[Open my] eye!" And immediately / he was able to see /51b with the other eye. And the two believed, and went away joyful, and they proclaimed throughout the whole country the miracle which had taken place.

Abba Aaron and the Miracle of the Child's Birth

124. 'And again, there was a certain God-fearing man in the city of Aswan. He was a believer, and came to visit us on numerous occasions. Now one day when he was thinking about coming to see us, his wife said to him, "If you're going to see the holy man Abba Aaron, entreat him to pray to Christ for us to give us a male child. I've heard that when it came time for a certain girl, she was unable to give birth, but when she called upon Abba Aaron in this matter, she gave birth to a son, but he was dead. Her father went to Abba Aaron and entreated him, and people say that when her father took a little dust from the door of Abba Aaron's house and threw it on the dead infant, he immediately came to life. With you, too, I believe that if you petition Abba Aaron, whatever you ask from him will come to pass."

125. 'So he came to us and related the story to my father, saying, "I have lived with my wife from the time I was a youth, and [we have had] no [male] child, [even after all these] years. Now, /52a therefore, [I believe that] God will grant you / [whatever you ask] from him." So the righteous one went to the place where he meditated alone, and he prayed in this way, saying, "My Lord, it was you who gave our father Isaac to Sarah when she was barren, and you gave Joseph to Gen 17:19, Rachel and you gave Samuel to Hannah. Now 30:22–24; therefore, Lord, what you were yesterday you are 1 Sam 2:21 also today; moreover, you are the same forever. I know your goodness, Lord. Please listen to my prayer and grant the petition of this man who has come to us."

126. 'When he had finished praying, he went to the man and said to him, "Go, my son, in the name of Christ. I believe that even as God said to our father Abraham, *I will come. Let it be* Gen 18:10 *time for Sarah to have a son*, it will also happen for you." And just as he had said, so it happened, and within a year the man came to us with his small son perched upon his shoulders. He held him out to my father, saying, "Look! The fruit which God has given to me through your holy intercessions." And the holy man Abba Aaron took him in his arms and praised God, saying, "Blessed are you, Lord, in all your works." Then he gave the child to his father, saying, "Behold God's favor which has come to you! May Christ who has graciously given him to you, my son, increase [him and] you, /52b / and may he enable us to do his will."

Abba Aaron and the Miracle of the Man Possessed by a Demon

127. 'Now again, there was a certain man whom a demon was wickedly tormenting. When his parents heard of Abba Aaron's fame, they

bound their son hand and foot and set him on a donkey and took him to Abba Aaron. Now it took four men to hold him. And when they had brought him, they lifted him off the donkey and set him down by the door. Now the demon was speaking from inside the man, hurling out many disgusting words to my father, saying, "Aren't you some soldier a long way from the slaughter? Weren't your family noble folk who ate up people with oppressive loans? I remember one day when your father loaned some guy ten oboli and when the man, because of his poverty, could not come up with the money to pay your father back, he seized his house in lieu of payment. Wasn't what he did a sin? And you—you've come here saying, 'I'm going to heal these sick people.' You're no doctor!"

128. 'Now my father restrained himself until the demon had finished everything he had to say. He said to him, "As for you, you don't deserve an answer. Now, therefore, I order you in the name of the crucified Christ to leave [this man]." When the demon heard [these words, he tried to] / take /53a the man and flee. Then the holy man filled his hand with water and sprinkled it on his face three times, saying, "In the name of the Holy Trinity, come out of him!" And the demon came out. The holy one said to him, "Get yourself to Babylon of the Chaldeans, and stay there until the day of judgement when everyone shall receive according to what he has done. As for you, you will be thrown into the pit of Amente."

129. 'When the demon heard these things, he left in a rage. Now when the man returned to his right state of mind, he glorified God, as did his parents and everyone accompanying them. Then they entreated the holy man to accept something, but he refused, saying that he had never accepted a gift of any kind since he had become a monk. (He was in the habit of telling me often, "Do not

set your gaze on the things of this world, which do not profit a person in any way, but as long as we have food and clothing, there will be enough for us. For indeed our Saviour said to his apostles, *Do not acquire for yourselves gold or silver or copper in your belts.* Therefore, it is fitting for a monk to walk / in this way and to lead a good life.") As a result, the parents renounced the world and followed the Lord.

Mt 10:9
/53b

Abba Aaron's Way of Life

130. 'Now it happened that after these things the holy man Abba Aaron rose and walked into the valley. As for me, he commanded me, saying, "Stay here. If anyone comes seeking me, say to him, 'He has gone to visit a brother.'" Now this was his ascetic way of life: When winter came he would soak his cloak in water and then put it on and stand in the chilly wet of the evening. He would spend the whole night praying, and when it was morning he would go into the crevices of the bitterly cold rocks. He gave himself no rest at all, either day or night. It was the same during the summer. He would stand in the burning heat and pray. He spent all of his time in the constant practice of this exacting ascetic way of life.

Abba Aaron and the Miracle of the Nile

131. 'Now it happened one year that the Nile did not rise enough to water all our fields, and a multitude of the poor came to him weeping and saying, "Our holy father, we and our children are going to die because the waters have not risen!" He said to them, "Believe [in God and he will deliver you. As it is written,] / *The prayer of the poor man who is downhearted, he pours out entreaty*

/54a

before the Lord. Again it says, *The Lord has heard the desires of the poor."* He quoted them numerous other passages from Scripture and explained them to them, and he comforted them and in this way they departed from him praising God. Now the holy man Abba Aaron was not unconcerned about their distress, and he would go to the river each evening and immerse himself in the water up to his neck and he would pray to God, saying, "My good Christ, compassionate one, have compassion upon your image and likeness". Indeed, he continued this practice until God had compassion for his tears and made the waters of the Nile flow over the face of the whole country.[73]

Ps 34:6?
Ps 12:5; 69:33

Abba Aaron and Another Miracle Concerning the Nile

132. 'Now it also happened one year that some men came to him filled [. . .] (as the narrative will show us if we continue on). Now they continued to entreat him to petition Christ to send them water <to save> the people. They were terrified because the proper time for the rising of the waters had passed. And they continued to weep [and beg the holy man. He had] compassion [on them and prayed to God,] / saying, "God, do not forsake the work of your hands, man and beast. For indeed you created us all from your blood and you deigned to come into the world. For our salvation you had a human birth. We know that with you nothing is impossible. God, do not forget the lives of the poor, lest they sin with their lips before you. For I remember what the wise man Solomon said, *Give me neither wealth nor poverty.* Whether God causes the waters to rise or not, it is for our refreshment alone. For God has the power to make all his creatures be in need

/54b

Pr 30:8

---

[73]For a comparable story, see the *Life of Pachomius* 100 (Veilleux, p. 137).

of their livelihood, but God allows the poor man to ask from the rich so that when the rich man shows mercy, mercy may be shown to him on the day of reckoning. Now the poor man, for his part, if he bears up under his poverty, he shall go into the kingdom [. . .] / the heavenly kingdom."

/55a

133. ' "The merciful person is like the ladder that Jacob saw: its foot was planted firmly on the earth while its top reached to heaven, and the angels of God supported it, that is to say, the Father of mercy. Consider that the Lord said *these little ones*, that is to say, those who are of little account. And again, as he said, *When you prepare a dinner or supper, do not invite your neighbors or your kin, but call the poor and the blind and the lame because they have nothing to offer you in exchange.*[74] *You will be rewarded at the resurrection of the righteous.* And even if you are not able to climb up to the top of the ladder, that is to say, if we cannot give in abundance, let us find the mercy that is perfect. Therefore, let us show mercy, for *mercy allows one to triumph over judgement."*

Cf. Gen 28:12

Mt 10:42, 18:6, 10, 14

Lk 14:13

Jm 2:13

134. 'Now when the holy man Abba Aaron had said these things, he prayed and dismissed them in peace, saying, "God will make the river fill with water, and he will bring it up to its proper level. Do not be afraid, and do not be unbelieving. You say that the time for the rising of the water has passed. Nevertheless, believe / that God has the power to do everything." And they got up and left in peace.

/55b

135. 'Now the following evening the holy one went to the river and prayed, saying, "Lord, you are the same yesterday, and today, and forever. It was you who burst open the rock and water flowed forth and you gave it to the people to drink. And when Samson was thirsty you caused

Ex 17:6

---

[74]There is a play on words in the text: the Coptic for what is translated as 'in exchange' is *toobou*; 'rewarded' is *toboou*.

the jawbone of an ass to bring forth water which quenched his thirst. Therefore, I entreat you today to send the river's water over the entire land so the poor among your people will have enough food and bless you and your holy name." And the holy man Abba Aaron spent the whole night praying and calling on God concerning the river's water. And so it was that the water rose and continued to rise, filling the river, and it did not subside for a day, until all of our fields had gotten water. And so there was abundance and plenty that year through the prayers of the holy man, as it is written, *The prayer of a righteous man is powerful and effective.* Jdg 15:19

Jm 5:16

Abba Aaron and the Blessing of the Poor Man

136. 'If we were to narrate all the wonders [that] God worked [through the prayers of the] holy man / Abba Aaron, this account would go on too long. Now it happened one day that he was sitting down with some people gathered around him. A poor man with a sack of barley on his back came to him and entreated him, saying, "Bless it for me, holy father, and I will go and make bread from it for my children, for I am a poor man." And the holy man Abba Aaron filled his hand with water and sprinkled it on the sack of barley, saying, "Go, and make bread for your children in the name of Christ. And he took the barley and left and made bread from it and a great blessing took place because of it. He returned to us glorifying God and the holy man Abba Aaron.

/56a

The Death of Abba Aaron

137. 'You see, my brother Paphnutius, I have told you a few things about the holy man Abba

Aaron's way of life. Because I am a tongue of flesh, it is impossible for me to do justice to his virtues. I will tell you the wondrous manner of his death. He was an old man, advanced in years. His body was worn out because of his severe ascetical practices. Now he got sick on the fifth of Pashons and on the following day, which was the sixth, I /56b heard the voices of a choir / of angels crying out, "Blessed, blessed". I did not know who they were talking about. (Now I, Paphnutius, said to him, 'This is his end. They are calling him blessed in heaven just as they blessed him on earth.') 'Now they continued in this fashion until the great [sic] first hour of the ninth of Pashons. And at the seventh hour of that day the holy man Abba Aaron died in very old age.[75]

138. 'We buried his body with honor and reverence. We laid him beside the bodies of the holy bishops who had been in Philae, that is, Abba Macedonius and Abba Mark and Abba Isaiah. Now, therefore, my brother Paphnutius, pray for me that God will have mercy on me and that he will make my end in this world pleasing to himself.' And I said to him, 'You are worthy of a great blessing, because from you I have heard of the monastic way of life of these holy men. Moreover, I for my part am going to write them down so that <they>[76] may be set down as authoritative models for all future generations.' And even so I have written them.

139. Now when we had finished talking with one another, I and Abba Isaac, [concerning] Abba Aaron, he prepared a table and we ate and drank /57a / together. We rose and prayed and I left him to go visit the brethren to his north.

---

[75]17 May.
[76]Text: you.

coda

140. This is the life of the holy man and anchorite of Philae, Abba Aaron, who completed his course in the desert to the east of Philae. Glory to the Holy Trinity, Father and Son and life-giving and consubstantial Holy Spirit, now and forever.

THE LIFE OF ONNOPHRIUS

THE LIFE[1] AND ASCETIC PRACTICE[2] OF OUR HOLY FATHER
ABBA ONNOPHRIUS THE ANCHORITE WHO WAS
GLORIOUS IN EVERY WAY, AND WHO ENDED HIS LIFE
ON THE SIXTEENTH OF PAONE IN THE PEACE OF GOD.
BLESS US.
AMEN.

1. A CERTAIN BROTHER, an anchorite by the name of Abba Paphnutius, narrated a story to the God-loving brethren, and these were the words that he spoke.[3]

Paphnutius Journeys into the Further Desert[4]

2. I, your brother, was thinking one day that I would go into the further desert so I could see whether there were any brother monks in the farthest reaches of the desert.[5] So I walked four days and four nights without eating bread or drinking water. I continued walking on into the farther desert when finally after a number of days I came upon a cave. / When I approached it, I /1b knocked at the mouth of the cave at midday, but no one answered me. Now I thought to myself, 'There's no brother here', but then I saw a brother sitting silently inside. I took hold of his arm and it

---

[1] Gr.: *bios*.
[2] Gr.: *poluteia*.
[3] For a story with a number of similar themes and topoi, see *Apophthegmata* Macarius of Egypt 2; Ward, 125–6.
[4] Paragraphing and section titles are the present translator's.
[5] Crum, *Coptic Dictionary* 343A, notes that 'brother monks' (Coptic: *son m̄monachos*) is used as a title in monastic narratives.

came off in my hands and disintegrated into dust. I felt his body all over and found that he was clearly dead and had been dead a long time. I looked up and saw a short-sleeved tunic hanging up.[6] When I touched it, it fell apart and turned into dust. I stood up and I prayed, and I took off my robe and wrapped the body in it. I dug with my hands in the earth; I buried him, and I left / that place.

/2a

Paphnutius Meets Timothy the Hermit

3. Now I walked on into the desert and I found another cave. I summoned up my courage[7] and I knocked at the mouth of the cave but no one answered me. I went inside, but did not find anyone. I came out, saying, 'This is where a servant of God lives; he will be coming home soon.' So I stayed there praying until late in the day and I was reciting Scripture I had learned by heart.[8] Now after the sun had set, I looked up and I saw a herd of antelope in the far distance coming towards me—with that brother right in the middle of them.[9] When he came near to me, he was naked and his hair covered his shame and served as clothing over him.[10] When he came up to me he got very scared, thinking that I was a spirit. / He stopped and prayed, for numerous spirits would tempt him, as he told me later.

/2b

---

[6]The short-sleeved tunic (Gr.: *kolobion*) was worn especially by monks.

[7]For students of english etymology, the Coptic is interesting here: literally, it is 'my heart came to me'. Compare with the French *cor*, 'heart', and the etymology of the English 'courage'.

[8]The Coptic has *apostethos* for the Greek *apostethismos*.

[9]See also ¶ 10 where Onnophrius is described in much the same terms: Timothy and Onnophrius would not be out of place in one of Henri Rousseau's 'edenic' paintings. On the theme of the return to Paradise, see S.P. Brock, 'Early Syrian Asceticism,' *Numen* 20.1 (1973), 11–12, and the references cited there. See also n. 44 below.

[10]The use of 'shame' (Gr.: *aschēmosunē*) for the genitals is biblical: see Ex 20:26; Dt 23:14; Lev 18:6ff.; Rev 16:15; Papias 3.

4. Now I perceived that he was afraid. I walked up to him and said to him, 'Why are you afraid, servant of God? Look, and you'll see by my footprints that I am a man. Touch me, and you'll find that I am flesh and blood.'[11] As he gazed at me he recited the Lord's Prayer.[12] I urged him to take me into the cave. He asked me, 'How is it that you've come to this place?' and I said, 'I came here because I wanted to see the servants of God who live in this desert, and God has not refused me what I was seeking.' I asked him, 'How is it that you came to this place? And how long has it been since you came here? What do you eat? And / why are you naked, without any clothes on?' /3a

The Story of Abba Timothy

5. Now he began to talk with me, saying: 'I was a monk living in a community of monks in the Thebaid. There came into my heart[13] a thought of this kind: "Rise and go, and stay in a place by yourself. You will lead a life of quiet contemplation as an anchorite.[14] You will welcome the brethren, you will show great hospitality to the stranger, and you will earn more than enough through the work of your hands." That which I thought, I did, so I left the community of monks. I built myself a dwelling and lived alone in it. A number of people gave me work to do and I gave the money in charity[15] to strangers.

---

[11]Cf. *Epistula Apostolorum* 11.
[12]Literally: the prayer of/in the Gospel.
[13]Or: mind.
[14]'Quiet contemplation' (Coptic *esuchaze* = Greek *heschazein*) could also be translated 'live as a hermit'. But the word *anachorei* (anchorite) which follows suggests this translation. For references to these words, see Lampe, *A Patristic Greek Lexicon* 608B (1b; 2a,b). The ideal of *hesychia* involved both solitude and quiet contemplation.
[15]Or: as alms. Coptic *na* is 'mercy, pity'; *mntna* is the abstract noun built on *na*.

Paphnutius

/3b

Cf. Jm 1:15

6. 'The Devil was jealous of me at that time because of the wages I was receiving before the Lord / on account of what I was doing for strangers and for others who were in need. Seeing how diligent I was in my work and what I was doing with what I earned, he grew very jealous of me and entered into a female monk.[16] She came to me and employed me to do a certain task. When I finished with it I gave it to her and she talked to me about doing further work. When it had become a regular thing for us to meet with each other, the Enemy put it into my heart to take more work from her. When we had become accustomed to talk freely, we ate bread together. The affair continued to grow until finally we gave birth to death and brought forth wickedness. And when I had fallen into folly with her we persisted

---

[16]Coptic *shimē mmonachē*. *Monachē* (Gr.) is the feminine form corresponding to the masculine *monachos*. For *monachē* in greek patristic literature, Lampe, 878B, cites only Theodorus Studita (d. 826). But see now E.A. Judge, 'The Earliest Use of Monachos for 'Monk,' " *Jahrbuch für Antike und Christentum* 20 (1977) 82. He cites a papyrus from Oxyrhyncus, dated to 400, which mentions two *monachai apotaktikai*. *Monachē* seems to be a rare word in the earliest monastic sources. The *Historia Monachorum* mentions nuns at least twice, at 5.6 and 14.4. In the first instance the bishop of Oxyrhyncus has 'under his jurisdiction 10,000 monks and 20,000 nuns'; in the second, a brigand rescues a nun from peril. The Greek in both of these cases is *parthenos*, 'virgin'. The *Life of Pachomius* 195, written in Bohairic Coptic, says that Theodore administered 'the other sex who are gathered together for the sake of God, that is, the nuns'. The Coptic for 'nuns' here is *nimonachē*. Unfortunately, the paragraph in which *monachē* appears does not occur in the First Greek *Life*. The modern Greek for 'nun' is *monachē*. In the fourth to fifth centuries it appears that the word for 'nun' was still fluid: both *parthenos* and *monachē* were used. The coptic sources suggest that the greek loan-word *monachē* was the preferred term in coptic monastic circles. Whatever its precise origin may have been, it seems clear that *monachē* came into use in Egypt in the fourth century, persisted as the word for 'nun' in Coptic, but did not achieve widespread use in greek-speaking Christianity until much later. For a philological and historical discussion of 'monk', see F.-E. Morard, 'Monachos, moine. Histoire du terme grec jusqu'au 4e siècle,' *Freiburger Zeitschrift für Philosophie und Theologie* 20 (1973) 332–411. Morard does not discuss *monachē*. For a recent discussion of women as sexual temptresses of monks, see Peter Brown, *The Body and Society: Men, Women and Sexual Renunciation in Early Christianity* (New York: Columbia University Press, 1988) 241–258.

in this wickedness for six months. After awhile I was reflecting in my heart about what I had done. I regretted it and wept bitterly / with sighs and groans.[17] I reflected in my heart when I was alone, saying, "If today or tomorrow I[18] were to die, I would be punished with a severe punishment, with the gnashing of teeth and the outer darkness, with the fire that cannot be quenched and the worm that never sleeps and devours the soul.[19] I must rise and leave this place and go into the desert." /14a

7. 'Now I was glad to flee from my sin. I rose and left and I came to this desert and I was never with that woman again. I found this spring of water and this date-palm tree and this cave. This palm-tree produces twelve bunches of dates each year, one bunch a month, and this one bunch / of dates is enough to last me for the month. Therefore I own nothing, neither clothing nor bread to eat. My hair continues to grow and since my clothes have completely worn out I clothe with my hair what should be respectfully covered. And, you see, it has been thirty years since I came here. The weather here offers me a uniform temperature and I eat no bread at all.' /4b

Timothy Tells of the Man of Light

8. I asked him, 'When you first came here, did you suffer a great deal?' He said to me: 'Yes, I suffered a great deal, my son, so much that I threw myself to the ground on account of my

---

[17]'I was reflecting...with sighs and groans' is mistakenly repeated in the text, dittography probably caused by the repetition of *aimeeue*, 'I reflected/was reflecting'.

[18]Text: we.

[19]Cf. Mt 8:12 and Mk 9:48, popular passages concerning judgement in coptic monastic texts.

pain and grief, crying out to the Lord on account of my many sins.[20] I also suffered great pain from an infirmity laid upon me. Now I looked and saw a man radiant with glory standing beside me.

/5a He said to me, / "Where are you sick?" And my strength returned to me a little and I said to him, "Sir, it's my liver that hurts me." He said to me, "Show me where it hurts". So I showed him where my liver was hurting me. He stretched out his hand over me, with his fingers joined together, and he cut open my side as with a knife. He brought out my liver and showed me the wounds in it. He healed them and bound them up and put my liver back in its place again, and he smoothed over the spot with his hands and rejoined the place which he had cut apart. He said to me, "See, you are healed. Do not sin again that no worse evil

Jn 5:14 happen to you. But be a servant of the Lord now
/5b and forever." Since that day / all my insides have been healthy and the pain in my liver has gone away. I have lived here in the desert without pain. And he taught me about the bindings which he treated me with.'

Paphnutius Leaves Timothy

9. I begged him to let me stay in the cave from where I had first seen him. He said to me, 'You are not strong enough to resist the attacks of the demons'. I begged him to tell me his name and he said to me, 'My name is Timothy. Remember me, my beloved brother, so that the Lord will allow me to finish the good fight to which he has called me.' I knelt down at his feet so that he might remember me and bless me, and he blessed me, saying, 'May the Lord bless you and keep you

---

[20]'So much...pain and grief' is mistakenly repeated.

from the snares of the Devil, and may he always set you on all his good paths, / so that you flee to the holy ones.' Now when he had finished blessing me, such strength came to me that I did not feel it at all when I was hungry or thirsty. When I saw the amazing thing that had happened to me, I rose and journeyed into the desert. /6a

Paphnutius, Strengthened by Timothy, Meets Onnophrius

10. When four days had passed I was worn out and I stretched out my hands to heaven and I prayed, and suddenly the man who had come to me the first time came to me again and he strengthened me as he had done the first time.[21] In short, four days later I journeyed on into [the mountain].[22] Now suddenly I looked and I saw a man in the distance; he was very terrifying because his hair was spread out over his body like a leopard's. Indeed, he was naked, and leaves covered his / male member. When he came up close to me I was afraid and I climbed up on a ledge of the mountain, thinking that perhaps it was a wild ass. Now when he came closer he threw himself down for awhile under the shadow of the mountain ledge; he was in great distress on account of the pain and suffering caused by hunger and thirst. He was in grave danger of dying. He raised his eyes to the mountain ledge; he saw me and called, 'Come down to me, holy man. I too am a man of the desert, like yourself. I live in this desert on account of my sins.' He said to me, 'You too are a friend of God'. So I sat down in front of him and I asked him to tell me his name. /6b

---

[21]The man: i.e., Timothy.
[22][the mountain]: missing from the text.

The Story of Onnophrius[23]

/7a 11. He said to me: / 'My name is Onnophrius, and for sixty years I have lived in this desert. I walk in the mountains like a wild beast and I never see anyone I recognize. Now I lived in a monastic community on the mountain of Shmoun in the Thebaid.[24] The name of that monastery was Eretē. We were all of one mind and lived in accord with one another, and peace dwelled in our midst. We lived together a life of quiet contemplation, glorifying God. Now I would spend the night in vigil with them, and I learned from them the rules of God. The great ones were perfect as the angels of the Lord are perfect. I heard them speaking about our father Elijah the Tishbite, saying that in every way he was powerful in God. There /7b lived in this / desert also John the Baptist: of those born of woman, none has arisen greater Cf. Mt 11:11 than he. He lived in desert places until the day of his manifestation to Israel. I said to them, "My fathers, aren't then those who live in the desert the elect—more so than we? Look, we see each other every day and we gather together for worship.[25] When we're hungry we have the benefit of food prepared for us; when we're thirsty we have the benefit of water to drink. When we're weak the brothers help us and when we want a plate or a pot to eat from we serve each other out of love for God. Where will those who live in the desert on account of God find anyone if they run into /8a trouble? / Or if they are hungry where will they find food; if they are thirsty where will they find water to drink?"

---

[23]For a story with many parallels to this one, see *Apophthegmata*, Macarius of Egypt 2, in Benedicta Ward, trans., *The Sayings of the Desert Fathers* (Kalamazoo: Cistercian Publications, 1975, 1984) 125–126.

[24]Budge, *Coptic Texts*, vol. 4, p. 460 n.1: 'The Egyptian Khemenu; i.e. the Hermopolis Magna of the Greeks, and the Ashmunen of the Arabs.'

[25]Worship: *sunaxis*.

Life of Onnophrius 153

12. '[They said to me,][26] "Indeed, when they begin their lives as anchorites they greatly rejoice on account of hunger and thirst and their agreeable manner of life.[27] Therefore the adversary, who fights against them to tempt them, does not want them to continue as anchorites because he knows that great is the reward which they will receive from God when they leave the body. Only when they endure do the mercies of God establish them. He causes the angels to serve them with food and he brings them water from a rock. For it is written in Isaiah: *Those who wait for the Lord will renew their strength, they will spread their wings like / the eagles. They will fly away and will not fall, they will journey and not be hungry.* He says, *They will receive water from a rock.* And again, *If they are hungry, he will make the grass in the field sweet in their mouths, as honey is sweet.* If trouble overtakes them or danger rises up against them, they immediately stretch out their hands and pray to Jesus the King until his help quickly comes to them. He speedily sends help and strengthens them on account of the uprightness of their hearts toward him. Have you not heard that which is written: *The Lord will not forsake his people, and the patient endurance of the poor man will not perish utterly*? And again, *The poor man cries out. The Lord hears him and rescues him from / all his afflictions.* God gives to each person according to what he has suffered. Blessed is he who will do the will of God on earth! I say to you that the angels will serve him from the moment of his birth and they will continue to comfort him at all times in his need."

Cf. Nb 20:11

/8b
Is 40:31, LXX
Cf. Is 48:21

?

Ps 9:9–12?
/9a
Ps 34:6

---

[26]The sense seems to require this, but the passage still seems muddled. The general sense is clear: those living as hermits are living a more holy life; Onnophrius leaves his monastery to seek them out.

[27]Agreeable manner of life: *polutia etthēt*. *Thēt* perhaps = Sahidic *tēt+*. See Crum, 437B, s.v. *tōt*.

Onnophrius Leaves the Monastery

13. 'And I, your brother, when I had heard these things from these perfect ones of God, they became like honey sweet to my soul[28] and I was filled within with complete understanding: I became like those whose minds travel to another world. I immediately got up; I took a few loaves of bread with me, sufficient for a journey of four days, so I would have something to eat until I reached the place which the Lord would determine for me. Now when I had left my monastery, /9b I looked and I saw a light / before me. I was afraid, and thought to myself that I would turn back to where I first had come and remain the way I was. When he saw that I was afraid, he said to me, "Do not be afraid. I am the angel who has dwelled with you and walked with you since you were a child. You will carry through to its completion this stewardship which the Lord has appointed for you."

Onnophrius Meets His Teacher

14. 'Now when I entered the mountain and had walked in the desert for six or seven miles, I saw a cave. I turned towards it because I saw that there was a person inside it. A great saint of God came out to meet me. He was handsome in appearance because his face shone with a great grace. When I saw him I knelt at his feet, but he raised me up and greeted me. He said to me, "You /10a are Onnophrius, my / fellow-worker in the Lord. Come in; the Lord be with you. You will succeed in the good work to which he has called you."

15. 'I went in, and I stayed with him for a few days. I learned from him about God[29] and

---

[28]Literally: sweet in my heart/mind.
[29]Literally: the rules of divinity.

he taught me how to do the works of the desert. When he saw that I understood the hidden and fearful fighting that takes place in the desert, he said to me, "Rise, let us go, my son. I am taking you to a desolate place in the further desert and you will live there by yourself for the sake of God. Since the Lord God has appointed you to this work, you must live in the desert." Immediately he rose and walked with me into the desert a four days' journey. At the end of four days we came to a small hut. He said to me, "This is the place which the Lord has appointed for you to live in." Now he dwelled / with me for a month of days   /10b
until I knew how to do the good work which it was right for me to do. Afterwards he left me and we did not see each other for a year until he laid down his body and I buried him where he had lived.'

Paphnutius Learns of the Ascetic Life of Onnophrius

16. I said to him, 'My good and beloved father, at the beginning when you first came to this place, did you suffer from the weather?' The blessed old man said to me: 'I suffered a great deal on numerous occasions from hunger and thirst and from the fiery heat outside during the day and the great frost at night. My flesh wasted away because of the dew of heaven. Now when God saw that I patiently endured in the good fight of fasting and that I devoted myself completely to ascetic practices, he had his holy angels / serve   /11a
me with my daily food; he gave it to me at night and strengthened my body. And the palm tree produced for me twelve bunches of dates each year, and I would eat one bunch each month.[30]

---

[30]Date palms in Egypt do not ordinarily produce fruit year round. I thank Professor Mohammed Gheith for confirming this.

And he also made the plants that grow in the desert sweet as honey in my mouth. For it is written, *A person shall not live by bread alone, but by every word which proceeds from the mouth of God shall* [Mt 4:4; Lk 4:4] *a person live.* If you do the will of God, he will care for you wherever you are, for he has said in the Holy Gospel: *Take no care for what you will eat or what you will drink or what you will clothe yourself* /11b *with. Your father in heaven knows what you need / without your asking him. Instead, seek his kingdom and his righteousness and these things will be added* [Mt 6:31–33] *unto you.*'

17. Now when I heard these things I was greatly amazed. I said to him, 'My holy father, where do you go for the eucharist on the Sabbath and the Lord's day?'[31] He said to me: 'My holy father, an angel of God comes and gives me the eucharist on the Sabbath and the Lord's day; and to everyone in the desert who lives[32] there on account of God and sees no human being, the angel comes and gives the eucharist and comforts them. What's more, if they desire to see anyone, they are taken up[33] into the heavenly places where they see all the saints and greet them, and their /12a / hearts are filled with light; they rejoice and are glad with God in these good things. Now when they are seen they are comforted and they completely forget that they have suffered. Afterwards, they return to their bodies and they continue to feel comforted for a long time. If they travel to another world through the joy which they have seen, they do not even remember that this world exists.'[34]

---

[31] Saturday and Sunday.

[32] *Poluteue* from Gr. *politeuein*. On *politeia* see pp. 17–18 above.

[33] Gr. *analambanein*, the same verb used in the Bible of Christ, Elijah, and Saint Paul, 'in a vision'.

[34] The text, with its use of two greek words, differentiates between 'worlds': the world that one travels to is designated by *aiōn*, whereas this world is called *kosmos*.

Onnophrius Takes Paphnutius to Live with Him

18. When I heard these things I greatly rejoiced that I was worthy to hear them from him, and I forgot all the sufferings I had undergone while I was journeying through the mountain. The strength returned to my body and youthful vigor returned to my body and soul. I said to him, 'Blessed am I that I have been worthy to see your holy face and hear your sweet words'. Then he said / to me, 'Rise, my brother, and /12b let us journey to where we will live'. We rose and journeyed together two or three miles. (A wonder to behold was the wonder of this blessed old man and athlete!) Now we walked and came to a hut and when we entered into the hut he stood and prayed with me. When we finished with the prayer, we gave the 'Amen', and we sat together and continued to talk about the greatness of God.

19. When the sun was about to set I looked and I saw a loaf of bread and a jar of water. He said to me, 'Rise, my brother; eat and drink this little bit of water, for I see that you are exhausted from hunger and thirst and the hardships of the journey.' I said / to him, 'As God Almighty lives, /13a I will neither eat nor drink unless we sit down and eat together.' Now when I continued to entreat him, he reluctantly agreed and so we sat down together. We divided the bread and ate and put some of it back; the two of us also drank from the jar of water and were satisfied and left some of the water in the jar. And we spent the whole night praying to God until morning.

Onnophrius Commissions Paphnutius

20. Now when morning came I saw that his face had changed and been transformed as though

he had become a different person: it[35] had turned completely into fire and his appearance greatly frightened me. But he said to me, 'Do not be afraid, my brother in God, for the Lord has sent you to care for my body and bury it. / Indeed, this very day I shall complete my stewardship and go to the place of everlasting rest.' (Now that day was the sixteenth of Paone.)[36] He also said to me, 'When you go to Egypt, proclaim my memory as fragrant incense to the brethren. Whoever makes an offering in my name and in memory of me, Jesus himself will bring him [into the feast][37] in the first hour of a thousand years.' But I said to him, 'If he is poor, he will not be able to make an offering in your name.' He said to me, 'Let him feed a poor brother in my name.' <I> said to <him>,[38] 'If he is poor, he will not be able to feed him. Will you not take him into the feast at the first hour of a thousand years?'[39] He said to me, 'Let him offer a little incense in my name.' But I said / to him, 'If he is poor he will not be able to offer incense in your name on account of his poverty. Come, my good father, let your grace rest upon us all, for whatever you ask from God, God will grant it to you.' He said to me, 'Let him stand and say his prayers three times to God in my name and the Lord Jesus will bring him to the thousand years and he will receive an inheritance with all the saints.'

21. Now I said to him, 'My holy father, if I am worthy, I wish to be by your holy side when you depart from this body.' He said to me, 'No, my son, for you have not been appointed to this stewardship, but the Lord has appointed

/13b

/ 14a

---

[35] Or: he.
[36] 10 June.
[37] Missing from the text; supplied from a similar sentence later on.
[38] Text: He said to me.
[39] The reference here to the 'thousand years' is to the Millenium; see Rev 20.

you to comfort the holy brothers who live in the desert, to proclaim their sweet fragrance among the brethren who worship God / as a benefit to those who listen to you. Now go to Egypt, my son, and persevere in the good work.' I immediately fell to the ground and said to him, 'Bless me, my father, that I may stand before God and as I have been worthy to see you on earth so may I be worthy to see you in the other world before the Lord Jesus Christ.' /14b

22. Now he said to me, 'My son, may God not cause you to grieve about anything and may he strengthen you in his love, so that your eyes may see the light of his divinity, that you neither turn away nor fall but succeed in the work which you have undertaken. May the angels shelter you and deliver you from the plottings of the Jews,[40] and may no accusation fall on you when you come to meet God.'

The Death of Onnophrius

23. When he had finished saying these things, / he rose and prayed to God with sighs and many tears. Afterwards he lay down on the ground and completed his stewardship of God, and he gave up his spirit into the hands of God on the sixteenth of Paone. And I heard the voices of angels singing hymns before the blessed Abba Onnophrius and there was great gladness when he came to meet God. /15a

24. Now I took off the cloak I was wearing and tore it in two: the one piece was for a burial shroud and with the other piece I covered myself so I would not stay naked. When I set his body down in a cleft in the rock, I heard the voices of a multitude of angels rejoicing and crying out,

---

[40]Meant symbolically?

/15b 'Alleluia!' I said my prayer over him and I rolled several stones over him. I stood / up and prayed a second time and immediately the palm tree fell down. Now I was greatly amazed at what had happened. I ate what was left of the bread and I drank the water that we had left.

Paphnutius Meets Timothy and His Companions

25. Now when I saw that it was not God's will that I remain there, I stretched out my hands and prayed to the Lord and suddenly the man who had come to me the first time and had strengthened me came to me again as he had done the first time. He said to me, 'Paphnutius, our Lord has informed me today that you were coming to us in this place. You are the first person we've seen in sixty years.' When we had spent some time talking with each other, finally <they> said to <me>,[41] 'Brother, strengthen yourself with a little bread, for you have come a great distance. The Lord /16a has determined that we are to remain / together for a few days and we will rejoice with you, our beloved brother.'

26. Now while we were talking together, five loaves of bread were brought in, warm and fresh as though straight from the oven; furthermore, in quick succession other dishes were brought in. We sat down and ate together and he said to me, 'See, we have been here sixty years, and four loaves of bread have been allotted to us each day, and these came to us from God. Now since you have come to us today, look, a fifth loaf has been brought for you. We have never known where they came from, but when we come in we find them sitting here.'[42]

---

[41] Text: we said to him.
[42] One should compare the *Historia Monachorum* 1.47 (Russell, p. 59): 'every two or three days [God] made a loaf appear on the table, a real loaf which could

Paphnutius is Sent to Egypt

27. When we finished eating together we spent the whole night in prayer until morning. When morning came, I entreated / them to let me stay /16b with them until the day of my death. They said to me, 'Our fellow-laborer, it has not been determined that you should stay here. Rather, rise and go to Egypt and tell those whom you see that the brethren here keep them in their thoughts, and it will profit those who listen.' Now I entreated them to tell me their names but they refused to say them. I tried to force them, but again they would not tell me their names. They answered and said, 'The one who has given names to everything and who knows everything, he is the one who knows our names. Now, then, our brother, remember us until we see you in the house of God. Be careful that you not allow the world to deceive you as it has done to so many.' When they finished saying / /17a these things, they blessed me and bid me farewell, and I left their mountain.

Paphnutius Discovers the Oasis and Meets the Four Monks

28. When I had traveled some days' distance from them, I came upon a well of water. I sat down for a little while because I was tired and

---

be eaten. And so whenever the monk felt the pangs of hunger and went into the cave, he found food.' A story similar to that of Onnophrius occurs in Jerome's *Life of Paul*. Paul and Antony meet and are talking about the state of the world: 'While they were chatting about such things, they watched a raven alight upon a branch of a tree. The bird then gently swooped down and dropped an entire loaf of bread before them as they sat marveling. Once the bird had flown away, Paul said, "Look, the Lord has sent us our meal. Truly, the Lord is gracious and compassionate. For sixty years now, I have received half a loaf, but now that you have come, Christ has doubled the ration for his soldiers."' See Paul B. Harvey, Jr., 'Jerome: Life of Paul, the First Hermit,' in Vincent L. Wimbush, ed., *Ascetic Behavior in Greco-Roman Antiquity: A Sourcebook* (Minneapolis: Fortress Press, 1990) 366.

there were large trees growing by the well. When I had rested awhile and slept a bit, I stayed there and walked among the trees. I was amazed and thought to myself, 'Who planted these here?' There were date-palms laden with fruit, and citron and pomegranate and fig trees and apple trees and grapevines, nectarine trees and kisma trees and other trees which gave off a sweet fragrance.[43] The well produced water and watered all the trees growing there.[44]

/17b   29. Now while / I was marvelling at the trees and looking at them and their fruit, suddenly four young men appeared in the distance, handsome in their appearance. They were dressed in fine sheepskin garments which they wore wrapped around them. When they came up to me they said to me, 'Greetings, Paphnutius, our beloved brother!' I prostrated myself at their feet and greeted them, but they raised me up and embraced me. They were very much at peace and were like those who come from the other world, so much joy and comfort did they bring to me. They set about gathering fruit from the trees and they placed it in my mouth. And as for me, my heart rejoiced because of the affection they showed toward me. I spent seven days with them eating fruit from the trees.[45]

---

[43]Nectarine trees: the coptic *dorakion* may be taken most easily as a metathesized corruption of Gr. *rodakinon*, 'nectarine.' *Kisma*, however, seems to be unattested; it is not Greek, although it may represent the greek ending -*kisma* (-*gisma*). Another coptic manuscript, in the Pierpont Morgan Coptic collection (M. 580) includes all the fruits listed here *except kisma*, an indication that the scribe of that ms could not understand the word, so he dropped it.

[44]This theme of finding a paradise on earth occurs frequently in early monastic sources; see Jerome's *Life of Paul* (Harvey, p. 362). For a discussion of the theme of paradise regained, see Peter Brown, *The Body and Society: Men, Women and Sexual Renunciation in Early Christianity* (New York, 1988) 218–24.

[45]Paphnutius and the four brethren have, at least symbolically, returned to Paradise and the original Garden, reversing Adam and Eve's sin of gluttony, restored to the original joy of creation.

The Story of the Four Monks

30. I asked them, 'Where have you come here from / and what region are you natives of?' They said to <me>:[46] 'Our brother, God has sent you to us so we can tell you about our whole manner of life, for we ourselves are natives of a city of Egypt called Pemje.[47] Our fathers were magistrates of the city and they sent us to school to have us educated. Now we were all in school together where we were like-minded fellows. When we had finished our education in the school we were sent to college. When we had been thoroughly and well educated in all the wisdom of this world, we then wanted to be instructed in the wisdom of God. Now it happened one day when we were talking together about these things, a good inspiration stirred us to action. / The four of us rose and set off into the desert so we could live in quiet contemplation until we saw what the Lord had determined for us. We took with us a few loaves of bread, enough for seven days.

31. 'Now when we had gone some distance into the desert, an ecstatic vision suddenly came upon us: a man, wholly of light, took us by the hand and brought us here. Now when we had come to this place we found a holy man of God, and the angel of the Lord entrusted us to him and for a year of days he set about teaching us to be servants of God. When the year was finished, the holy and blessed old man died and we remained alone here. Our noble brother, we confess to you in the Lord that it has been sixty years and we have not known the taste / of bread or any other kind of food except the fruit from these trees which we live on. When we wish to see each other we gather here each week to see one another. We

/18a

/18b

/19a

---

[46]Text: him.
[47]Oxyrhyncus.

spend the whole night of the Lord's day together and afterwards each of us goes and lives his own ascetic life.'

Paphnutius Learns of the Ascetical Life of the Four

32. I said to them, 'Where do you gather for the eucharist?' They said to me, 'We assemble right here for that purpose, and every Sabbath an angel of God comes and gives us Communion on the Sabbath and on the Lord's day.' Now I stayed with them and greatly rejoiced. [They said to me,] 'On the seventh day of the week an angel of the Lord will give Communion to us and to you together, and the person who receives Communion from the hand of that angel will be /19b washed clean / from all sin and the adversary will in no way have power over him.'

33. Now while we were talking together I smelled a powerful fragrance whose like I had never smelled. As soon as the fragrance washed over us we got up and stood and praised God. Afterwards the angel came and gave us Communion together by means of the body and blood of the Lord. Now because of the fearful sight I had seen I became like those who are asleep. The angel blessed us and ascended into heaven as we watched him with our eyes. When he had gone, they brought me to my senses and said to me, 'Be strong and resolved and be a person of determination.'[48] Immediately I became soberminded like those recovering from the influence of wine.[49] And we spent the whole night of the /20a Lord's day / standing and praying until morning.

---

[48]Compare this scene with that of Jesus' transfiguration (Lk 9:28–36).

[49]This seems to be the sense required. Or, if one translates 'like those under the influence of wine', perhaps it refers to a mystical 'sober intoxication', a meaning certainly not at odds with the mystical content of the narrative. See Philo, *Quod omnia probus liber sit* 13.

Paphnutius is Sent by the Angel to Egypt

34. Now when the light appeared at dawn on the Lord's day, we suddenly smelled that sweet fragrance once again. We took delight[50] in it and rejoiced like those in the other world. Afterwards the angel came and gave us Communion, and he blessed each one of us, saying, 'Life everlasting shall be yours, and imperishable prophecy'. And all of us at the same time and with one voice cried out, 'Amen! So be it!' Afterwards the angel turned to me and said to me, 'Rise and <go>[51] to Egypt and tell the God-loving brethren what you have seen, so they may emulate the way of life of the holy ones.' I entreated him to let me remain / with them, but he said to me, 'The Lord /20b does not assign to us the work that we want to do, but God gives to each person what he can bear. Now, then, rise and go, for that is what the Lord has determined for you.' And he blessed me and ascended to heaven in glory.

35. Now they brought a large quantity of plums[52]. We ate together and I left them. They accompanied me for about six miles, and I entreated them, saying, 'Tell me your names'. Now they told me their names, each one of them. The first was John, the second was Andrew, the third was Heraklamon, the fourth was Theophilus. And they commanded me to tell their names to the brethren so they could be remembered. And I for my part entreated them to remember my name. And we prayed and said goodbye / to one another. /21a
I began my journey and was very sad, but because of the blessing which the holy ones had given me, I rejoiced.

---

[50]Coptic *hēdane* = Gr. *hēdunesthai*, influenced by Gr. *handanein*. Cf. *Nag Hammadi Codices* IX,3, *Testimony of Truth* 68,3 and note.

[51]Text: rise.

[52]Coptic *hupora* = Gr. *opōra*. See *LSJ* 1243A. See *LSJ* Supplement 146A for *hupora* as a variant for *opōra*, a reading found in the Oxyrhyncus papyri.

Paphnutius Comes to Egypt

36. Now after a journey of three days I came into Egypt, and when I found the God-loving brethren, I rested with them for ten days. I told them what had happened to me and they said to me, 'Truly you have been worthy of a great gift.'[53]

coda

37. Now those brothers were lovers of God and champions, worshipers of God with their whole heart. They lived in Scetis. They hurriedly wrote down these words which they heard from Abba Paphnutius. They quickly put them in a book and sent it to Scetis where it was placed in the church for the benefit of those who heard it. And they spoke about it and it was the topic of /21b conversation[54] in the mouth / of everyone as they glorified God and praised his holy ones through the grace of our Lord Jesus Christ and his love for humankind, to whom be the glory,
        and to his good Father
        and to the Holy Spirit
        for ever and ever.
        Amen.

---

[53] Coptic *hmot*, 'grace, gift, favor'.
[54] Or: 'study, meditation'; Gr.: *meletēsis*.

PISENTIUS OF COPTOS
A DISCOURSE ON SAINT ONNOPHRIUS*

INTRODUCTION

THIS DISCOURSE (*logos*) or homily, 'considered one of the best of its kind, not only in Coptic letters but in the whole range of Christian literature',[1] tells us virtually nothing about the historical Onnophrius.[2] Yet it reveals a great deal about its preacher, Pisentius, and about his congregation and his times. The occasion for the address is the feast day of Saint Onnophrius. The site was probably a church dedicated to the famous ascetic and anchorite not far from Pisentius' episcopal see at Coptos (Qift or Keft).[3]

Pisentius (in Greek, Pisenthios), a famous pastor and preacher, and 'among the most outstanding personalities of the Coptic church', was born in 568–69 in the district of Hermonthis in the Thebaid of Upper Egypt, just upriver from Thebes

---

*I wish to thank Jeffrey Russell and Severus Mikhail for their suggestions.

[1] C. Detlef G. Müller and Gawdat Gabra, 'Pisentius, Saint', *The Coptic Encyclopedia*, ed. Aziz S. Atiya (New York: Macmillan, 1991) 6:1978–80; the quotation is on 1979.

[2] W. E. Crum, ed. and trans., 'Discours de Pisentius sur Saint Onnophrius', *Revue de l'Orient Chrétien*, ser. 2 10:20 (1915–1917) 38–67, notes, 41, how vague the references to Onnophrius' ascetic practices are in the discourse and observes that they could apply equally well to all other monastic heroes.

[3] Müller and Gabra, 1979; Crum, 40–41.

(modern Luxor).⁴ At the age of seven he entered the monastery and for the next twenty-three years lived in various monasteries of the Thebaid. In 598, when he was thirty, he was consecrated bishop of Coptos, which lies on the east side of the Nile, halfway between Thebes to the south and Tabennisi, the site of the famous pachomian monastery, to the north. Pisentius had a long episcopacy of thirty-three years, and died in July 632, just a few years before the muslim conquest of Egypt (641).

At about the time of Pisentius' birth just a few years after the death of Emperor Justinian (d. 565), a remarkable debate on the origin of the world took place in Alexandria between John Philoponos and Cosmas Indicopleustes. This learned and literary exchange in Greek 'pitted a literate, observant, and intelligent merchant [Cosmas] against one of the most outstanding teachers of philosophy [John]', and demonstrates the deep symbiosis between christian and ancient learning that still obtained in that cosmopolitan city far to the north of the Thebaid.⁵ By contrast, Pisentius' concerns are, quite literally, parochial. Although he probably knew Greek, he composed his homily in Coptic, the language of his congregation.⁶ Pisentius was speaking not so much to his hearers' minds and intellect as he was to their hearts.

Preachers preach, but as preachers both ancient and modern know, while they are preaching the stomachs of their parishoners rumble and members of the congregation nod off and look out the window. Origen complains about people talking and milling about during one of his sermons, and a sixth-century preacher in Palestine confesses to counting candles, pew seats, and planks in the roof during the divine liturgy.⁷ Any writtem document reveals a multitude of worlds, and worlds within worlds; along with the theological cosmos that Pisentius pre-

---

⁴For the details of his life, see Müller and Gabra, 1979–80 (the quotation is on 1978), and for sources see the bibliography on 1980.

⁵For the story, see Judith Herrin, *The Formation of Christendom* (Princeton: Princeton University Press, 1987), 87–89; the quotation is on 87.

⁶This is Crum's conclusion, 41–42.

⁷'An Encomium on The Life of Saint Theognius', 24, translated by William Morison and Tim Vivian in Tim Vivian, *Journeying into God: Seven Early Monastic Lives* (Minneapolis: Fortress, 1996) 163–64.

sents, there exists another, more pedestrian, world of seventh-century habits and predilections, deeds and misdeeds. For the modern reader, this is the sociological or historical subtext for the main theological text. Or, perhaps, if we take ourselves less seriously than we are wont to do, we can see both Pisentius and ourselves with a sense of humor and view this subtext as the comic relief which serves as counterpoint to the main drama. The grave diggers in *Hamlet* provide comic relief, but they also have important things to say. As we read this sermon we can imagine ourselves looking through the window of the church dedicated to Saint Onnophrius, watching Pisentius deliver his discourse and observing the pilgrims who have come to pay homage to one of the great saints of the egyptian Church. For Pisentius—as we will see in detail below—the purpose of observing the feast day is the encouragement of moral and ethical emulation: 'Let each of us', he urges, 'pay careful attention to the way of life of this blessed saint . . . at whose holy shrine we gather today as we observe his holy feast day, so that you may in this way show that you have conformed yourselves to his faith and upright life.' Yet in addition to moral exhortation, Pisentius offers us, almost inadvertently, details about feast days and pilgrimage in the sixth and seventh century, and about what his listeners did at their devotions—or at least what he expected them to do.[8]

First, the pilgrims walked, and did not drive, to the shrine. This obvious fact may seem unimportant, but we must remember that walking takes more time than driving. In Pisentius' opinion, the journey allowed opportunity for improper and irreverent behavior, especially among the women. According to the bishop, they clapped their hands, sang, and flirted. Women, he insists—before the influence of Islam was felt in Egypt—, should cover their heads and bodies, both in church and on the streets of their village. Before the pilgrims begin their trek, the bishop urges, they should pray at home, asking God to 'make straight their path'. While they are on the road, they are to continue praying and recounting the lives of the saints. This, he hopes, will help them avoid distractions along the

---

[8]See David Frankfurter, ed., *Pilgrimage and Holy Space in Late Antique Egypt* (Leiden: Brill, 1998).

way. When the pilgrims arrive at the shrine, he urges, they should not loiter but go straight into the church, pray to the saint, and keep vigil through the night: 'fighting against drowsiness by saying holy psalms and giving the responses to those who are singing psalms'.

Distractions, however, come easily. Pisentius exhorts the pilgrims to be attentive and not to speak idle words to their neighbors. He forbids them to 'leave the church to sit by the door and speak vain and empty words in whispered conversation'. This admonition tells us that all was not silence and contemplation. In addition to the silence Pisentius hopes for, the vigil required fasting: 'do not drink or eat anything at all until you have received Communion and heard the deacon say "Go in peace"' at the end of the service. Apparently the pilgrims kept vigil throughout the night and celebrated the Eucharist in the morning. Pisentius' address appears to have been, not a sermon during the eucharistic liturgy, but an exhortation given at the beginning of the observances. Apparently, too, the pilgrims brought along their children; one wonders how they—both parents and children—managed an all-night vigil!

After the observances, Pisentius urges the people to return home in the spirit of the feast day and the embrace of the saint: they are to eat modestly, give a portion of their bread to the poor, and 'continue [praying] day and night'. Pisentius was keenly aware that his words might be falling on deaf ears; he admits to having a feeling that he has 'saddened' some of his congregation with his hard words. He also has the preacher's great fear of 'out of church, out of mind': 'Yes, I exhort you, do not listen to these words only to discard them behind you; do not leave them in the church where they were read to you, emptied of their power, while you leave' and head for home. Where there is homiletical smoke, there is undoubtedly behavioral fire. These details are amusing, but they do not mock, or even detract from, Pisentius' message; they give flesh and blood both to the preacher and to his flock. Fourteen centuries later, we can still see the very human villagers walking the dusty road to the shrine, the girls giggling and singing songs; we can see some of the worshipers letting their attention wander, and others congregating outside to talk, as I have seen men in Greece do still today. On this holy feast day, we can see the preacher ascend the stone steps of the pulpit (a pulpit from Pisentius' century survives in the Coptic Museum in Cairo);[9] there he addresses the pilgrims on the meaning of holiness and the means of salvation.

For Pisentius, the surest path to God lay in the emulation of the saints, especially saints like Onnophrius, 'the guide toward all that is good'. There is nothing in this homily specifically *about* Onnophrius, what we call the 'historical' person: no stories, no sayings, no ascetic feats, no healings, no miracles. Yet the bishop insists that each person should 'be zealous for the way of life of this righteous man and saint... his life is instructive for each generation'. We might at first be inclined to think that this is a terribly abstract and awfully vague saint, a simulacrum of the flesh-and-blood ascetic. But we need to remember that Saint Paul was not very concerned with the 'historical' Jesus. His focus was on the risen Christ. In the same way, for Pisentius it was Onnophrius transfigured who mattered, Onnophrius as the embodiment of flesh and blood's greatest potentiality—and more than possibility—: human perfection.

For Pisentius, what is imperfect is, through God's grace, on its way to perfection. If young people keep themselves pure, they 'will come to resemble the righteous one'. If rulers render 'just [*dikaios*] judgement' to all concerned, they imitate 'the way of life of the righteous [*dikaios*] Abba Onnophrius'. 'If someone opposes you and provokes you... remember the patience of the saints'. If the wealthy give to the poor and refrain from being usurious, they 'too will become as wise as the saints: having fixed your sights upon the exalted nature of their good way of life, you have become like them'. Imitation is, indeed, the sincerest form of divine flattery: 'the saints love especially those who have emulated their [lives]... and they seek them out in order to save them from their sins'.

Living saints may have been becoming scarce in Egypt during the lifetime of Pisentius, and so it was the blessed dead who provided the best exemplars of life in Christ:

---

[9]See Gawdat Gabra, *Cairo: The Coptic Museum and Old Churches* (Cairo: Egyptian International Publishing Co.—Longman, 1993), 64–65.

> In the earlier period of the history of Nitria and Scetis, pilgrims made their way into the desert to be edified by the discourse of the fathers, to beg for their prayers, and to receive their blessing. . . . In the seventh century a change seems to have come over both pilgrims and monks. The former seek out holy places believing that prayer there will, through the mediation of some departed saint, lead to a cure or to some other benefit; the latter are drawn more and more to realize the advantages presented to them by such an attitude, and come to look upon relics as an attraction bringing renown and wealth to their monastery. In proportion, then, as the sanctity of the living grew less remarkable, the veneration of the dead increased.[10]

What matters here is not so much religious change as religious reality. Pisentius is nothing if not a realist. He catalogues humankind's besetting sins and failures and upbraids his flock for lust, fornication, acquisitiveness, greed, gluttony, drunkenness, and—like a dour puritan—singing, dancing, joking, and merrymaking. We may smugly chuckle at these last vices—as at Pisentius' repeated fulminations against women—but if we understand how they fit into his theology, we may see why they mattered so much to him. Pisentius was a monk, and in his homily he evinces the monk's dread of distractions, those diversions that literally drag us away from God. For this monk-bishop, the evil twin of distractions is indifference, lack of concern (*amelês* in Greco-Coptic), what we today call apathy and self-centeredness. The besetting sin in this is indifference to others, to God and, ultimately, to salvation. Pisentius shrinks in horror from this.

For Pisentius, to be indifferent is to reject God's mercy and compassion (the single coptic word *na* encompasses both). God 'loves us', and God's 'desire is to have compassion' (Is 54:8); God wants us to be 'a holy nation and people worthy of life' (1 Pt 2:9; Ex 19:6); God has reconciled us and saved us and

---

[10]Hugh G. Evelyn White, *The Monasteries of the Wadi 'N Natrun* (3 vols.; repr. New York: Arno Press, 1973) 2:292.

given us 'the grace of his mercy'. With this reminder of these beliefs the homily ends. These facts are for Pisentius a prevenient reality. All the other things we lust after and prize, he repeatedly emphasizes, are fleeting, passing, ephemeral. God's reality is grounded most visibly and palpably in the saints; he presents this to his flock most clearly in a theological syllogism that has profound ethical implications: 'if the remembrance of the saints abides in our souls at all times, we will say with the holy psalmist David...: "I have kept the Lord before me at all times...."' And if we have God before us at all times, 'we will never incline toward sin'. Given human nature, this is a faith that believes in moving more than mountains.

A DISCOURSE ON SAINT ONNOPHRIUS[11]

A DISCOURSE PROCLAIMED BY... ABBA <PISENTIUS>, BISHOP OF THE CITY [OF KEFT].[12] HE PROCLAIMED IT AT THE COMMEMORATION OF THE PERFECTED ONE AND TRUE HERO OF CHRIST, <SAINT> ABBA ONNOPHRIUS THE ANCHORITE AND PERFECTED HERMIT.

In the peace of God. Amen.

The holy apostle, the teacher Paul, the tongue of incense,[13] established a law for us that we should remember[14] our forefathers,[15] those who spoke the word of God for your benefit: consider the exalted nature of their way of life and <imitate their faith>[16]... despise God's law and find a pretext there not to emulate the saints, saying these things while making excuses when they say, 'We have [14 lines lost]'.[17]... wish... to please him... times of old. Moreover, he is the same God today, for he has not changed, nor has he been transformed,[18] but he is ready to strengthen everyone who wishes to be chosen [8 fragmentary lines follow] and lovers of Christ.

Since you have obeyed the commandment of the apostle who has commanded us to continue to remember, as he said, 'Remember your forefathers who spoke the word of God for your benefit', you have, therefore, [5 lines missing] Abba

---

[11]The translation is based on the Sahidic Coptic text edited by Crum, 43–57. Crum also supplies a French translation. For this translation, I have not reproduced all the bracketing and sublinear dotting of Crum's text, indicating with brackets only those words for which there is no extant text and for which either Crum or I have made conjectures.

[12]Keft, or Qift, is the ancient Coptos.

[13]'Incense' (literally: 'good smell'), *stinoufe*, and 'Onnophrius', *ouanofre*, are related etymologically: *noufe*, 'good' < *nefr-*, 'be good, profitable'.

[14]In Coptic, as in English, 'remember' and 'commemorate' are related etymologically.

[15]Coptic *nos* also indicates 'the great ones', 'elders'.

[16]Heb 13:7.

[17]Possibly a reference to or quotation of Mt 3:9: 'Do not presume to say to yourselves, "We have Abraham as our ancestor"; for I tell you, God is able from these stones to raise up children to Abraham.'

[18]See Si 42:21.

<Onnophrius> on the <day> of his holy commemoration. Let us obey the text that follows afterwards, which says, 'Imitate their faith', for in saying 'Imitate their faith', it is these <saints> whom... we imitate by these <words (?)> [5 fragmentary lines] the faith... and the guide toward all that is good. 'Without faith, it is impossible to please God';[19] without faith... a person cannot [begin (?)] to do good [9 fragmentary lines] a person cannot... nor... the good... his reward from God.

Therefore, my beloved children, let each person be zealous for the way of life of this righteous man and saint, Abba Onnophrius the anchorite, beloved of God and humanity.... God [4 lines missing] each one love the life that endures. For his life is instructive for each generation, for people of all ages, whether male or female. If we are unable to renounce the world and its vain and fleeting concerns, and we lose our lives on account of this world,[20] as... blessed <Abba> Onnophrius, whose feast day we celebrate today so that we... live... according to the word of Christ that does not lie. But let us imitate his holy life, each one of us according to his own ability.

I want to tell you, my beloved children, that in whatever way we are able to imitate the life of that mighty man, Saint Abba Onnophrius... young people, those who are in the rank[21] of youth, and the young girls whose bodies are young with ephemeral youth, keep your holy bodies in all purity so that you may truly become <the> children of this holy one in the kingdom of heaven. But when you see the thought [4 lines missing] quickly remember the struggles and the way of life of this righteous man, and you yourselves fight against sin as he did: flee evil thoughts, guard your undefiled purity in freedom and sobriety and complete confidence until you <are joined together>... marriage... God [3.5 lines missing]. In this way, through the purity of your flesh and your purified

---

[19] Heb 11:6.
[20] See Mt 16:26.
[21] Coptic/Gk: tagma. In the early Church the Church was often thought of as consisting of many ranks or orders: for example, widows, virgins; later, married, celibate, lay, clergy.

hearts,[22] you will come to resemble the righteous one.[23] That is to say, let the husband watch over his wife, and let the wife do likewise for her husband,[24] and you will do what is righteous in everything you do: you will yourselves conform your life to the life of <this saint>.

And you, you who rule over others, when you see someone being mistreated and you render a just judgement on all sides, in this you will become one who imitates the way of life of the righteous Abba Onnophrius;[25] furthermore, you will become a co-inheritor with all the saints. On the other hand, you who are well off with the means of life of this world and in the goods that you possess for a short time, when you <give> to the person in need and do not dun the person in debt to you, and when you withdraw your hand from receiving burdensome interest and feed the poor whom the Lord has given you, you too will become as wise[26] as the saints: having fixed your sights upon the exalted nature of their good way of life, you have become like them.

But if someone opposes you and provokes you, you for your part should remember the patience of the saints: be patient yourself, bear with the person who afflicts you. Although you have the power to pay him back, do not do so; no, you have heeded the holy commandment that commands you, 'Do not repay anyone evil for evil'.[27] You then, for your part, are a person who by your patience conforms himself to the saints. You also have the power to... to others for evil, <according> to the word of our father David who boasted, saying to the Lord, 'If I have paid back those who have done evil to me, then let me fall destitute at the hands of my enemies'.[28] Let each of you, my beloved children, pay careful attention to the way of life of this blessed saint who acts as a judge in the contest, <this> true athlete who fought well, Abba

---

[22]Crum's text, 45 l. 13, misprints *hmt forhêt*.
[23]This section might well be a response by Pisentius to Ps 119:9: 'Can young people keep their way pure?'
[24]See Eph 5:33.
[25]'Just' and 'righteous' both render *dikaios*.
[26]Coptic/Gk: *philosophei*.
[27]Rom 12:17.
[28]See Ps 7:4.

Onnophrius the anchorite, at whose holy shrine[29] we gather today as we observe his holy feast day, that you may in this way show that you have conformed yourselves to his faith and upright life.

Your gathering at his holy shrine brings no honor to the righteous one if you do the things that he hates. The honor of the saints surpasses every honor on earth, for the saints do not love jokesters or mockers or drunkards or those who clap their hands like idiots or dancers, and all the rest of these disgraceful rogues. But the saints love especially those who have emulated their <lives> and have joyfully followed them, and they seek them out in order to save them from their sins so they may repent. For they love those who observe their fasts at all times without blemish; they love those who pray to God with a pure heart;[30] they love those who keep their marriage holy and pure;[31] they love those who keep their virginity holy and pure in their parents' house. Truly, these are the ones whom the saints seek out, and they want them to gather at their holy shrines. The righteous one will not consent that you honor him with your mouth alone while you say to him 'My father and my lord, holy and righteous', as you continue to abide in the things that he hates. In the same way, the Lord did not put up with those who honored him only with their mouths;[32] as he reproachfully said to them, 'Why do you call me Lord when you do not do what I tell you?'[33]

If, then, you wish to honor the righteous one, honor him with the purity of your body, for the righteous Abba Onnophrius, whose feast day we celebrate today, made his life perfect with hunger and thirst and vigils in the night. But you who are listening to me, even if you are not ever able to fast until the ninth hour,[34] fast at least during the forty holy days[35] and twice each week, and be satisfied with a little wine in

---

[29]Literally: place (*topos*), and throughout.
[30]See Mt 5:8 and 2 Tm 2:22.
[31]See perhaps Heb 13:4.
[32]See Mt 15:8 (Is 29:13).
[33]Lk 6:46.
[34]Roughly 3 PM.
[35]Lent is first attested by Athanasius in 334 in *Festal Letter* 6.13; see also *Festal Letter* 13.8 and Egeria, *Diary of a Pilgrimage* 27–29.

moderation and with enough food to meet your needs—and do not mercilessly amass money![36]

But you, you who are indifferent[37] to others, who have come to the shrine of the saints: if you are a fornicator; or if you are a . . .; or if you deceitfully. . . your neighbor, doing evil to him; or if you act wickedly with regard to your neighbor's goods, taking them from him; or if you hate him; or if you envy him with bitter jealously; or if you pervert justice to your neighbor's detriment for the sake of a gift; or if you converse with idle words, using filthy language; if, then, you are people of this sort and you do <such things>, you who have come to the shrine of the saints, then you have come in vain, for the saints hate people who do such things, and they will refuse to appear in your presence—especially since one of you has done such things while you[38] have assembled at their holy shrines!

If you enter into a worldly business dealing, you who are listening to me, you undoubtedly zealously and carefully negotiate every aspect of your business, not only in order not to suffer a loss, but also in order to make a profit from your business. And if you return just as you left, without making any profit, the matter weighs very heavily on you, especially if you suffer a loss in the things that you took with you when you had expected to double them; as a result, you will be very sad for a long time. If, then, you have this great zeal, you fool, for things that will perish in a little while—things that can not offer you any help, nor can you take them with you where you are going—then[39] how much more appropriate is it for you to be zealous for business that is truly spiritual, and acquire *it*! For the businessmen of the kingdom of heaven are the saints; and the violent, those who steal, are those who do violence to their own souls on account of the vain and

---

[36]'Mercy', *na*, 'pity, compassion', will be an important theme later in the homily.
[37]'Indifference, lack of concern', especially for others, Gk *amelês*, is an important theme of the discourse; see the introduction. See also n. 94 below.
[38]Text: they.
[39]Reading with Crum *eie* instead of *ê*.

empty things of this world.⁴⁰ Consider, therefore, each of you, the life of this righteous man and truly holy athlete, Abba Onnophrius, and understand how he became a rich man in the kingdom of heaven which endures for ever. You, too, should be zealous to become rich in the same way in the kingdom of heaven, which endures for ever.

Take care, therefore, my beloved and my children, as you gather at the places of the saints on the day of their holy commemoration, that you who are gathering here to receive a blessing not receive a curse in place of a blessing!⁴¹ Take care, therefore, my beloved children, to be wise in all things, either with regard to what you see with your eyes, or with regard to your conduct, or your conversation. Moreover, let the women not walk with a haughty look,⁴² or shamelessly gaze with their eyes into any man's face, or walk with their faces uncovered, not only here in church, but also on the streets of your village. For you women know that I have warned you many times with regard to these commandments,⁴³ and you have refused to desist from your madness! But now I write once more, exhorting you, and I strongly command you with a great commandment, that no woman at all is to go out of the doors of her house with her head uncovered, nor raise her eyes to the face of any male stranger at all. Rather, you women are to walk at all times with your <eyes> lowered to the ground and with your clothing covering every part of your body in complete freedom,⁴⁴ and when you adorn yourselves, it is fitting that you do it with moderation⁴⁵ and do it in a seemly manner, devoting yourselves at all times to the word of God with great devotion, thirsting for it at all times.

---

⁴⁰As Crum notes, 61 n. 1, Pisentius seems to be offering an interesting exegesis of Mt 11:12.
⁴¹See Gn 27:12.
⁴²See Si 26:9.
⁴³See 1 Cor 11:5.
⁴⁴See 1 Tm 2:9. Crum, 61 translates *hn mnteleutheros* as 'en toute bienséance', 'with all decency', 'seemliness', or 'modesty', which fits the context, but I cannot find that meaning for Gk *eleutheros*. 1 Tm 2:9 does say (NRSV) that 'women should dress themselves modestly', but 'modestly' there renders Gk *sôphrosunês*, not *eleutherias*.
⁴⁵Literally: a measure of justice.

Moreover, teach your sons good behavior also,[46] and teach your daughters to stay at home and be with their husbands, for it is instruction from parents that raises children in freedom.[47] But when children are instructed in weakness, as Eli did with his,[48] it causes a lack of faith to take root and flower. But you husbands who are obedient and lovers of Christ, command your children to walk in all wisdom, for you know that I will not cease instructing you and commanding you about this. Do not permit them to occupy themselves with distractions that do them no good, or with idle words[49] that do them no good, or with mischief-making music; do not let them keep company with those who beat sticks together,[50] as the ignorant are accustomed to do, or with musicians, or with anyone who does things of this sort. A child who is distracted all the time sharpens a knife to use against himself. Pay attention here! I assure you, my children, that the person who neglects his child when the latter falls into fornication, who has not taught his child in such a way that the child turns and repents, this parent receives his condemnation in this world, <and>[51] in the next the soul that sins will die, according to what is written.[52]

Do not, then, my beloved children, do not tolerate the doing of these disgraceful things that do no one any good, and that applies especially to idle words, lest we provoke God on account of our wicked deeds. Instead, Christians, know the proper way to observe the feast day of the saints,[53] lest we too hear what was said through the holy prophet, who says to us: 'I will turn your feasts into mourning',[54] and again, 'I hate

---

[46] Literally: to walk well.
[47] Reading *eutheros* as *eleutheros*, as does Crum, 61. See n. 44 above.
[48] See 1 Sam 2:27–36.
[49] Or, perhaps, songs, singing; Crum translates *henjô* (in French) as 'chants'.
[50] This phrase is not clear (see Crum 62 n. 1), but seems to suggest percussive music-making. I am grateful to Birger Pearson for his advice on this sentence.
[51] Crum recommends, 50 n. 1, adding 'and'.
[52] See Ez 18:4.
[53] Reading with Crum *nechristianos enetouaab* (= *nnetouaab*) instead of *nechristianos etouaab* ('Know, O Christian saints... the feast day...'),
[54] Am 8:10.

your feasts, I turn away from them',[55] and 'I will not look upon your revelations at your great feasts',[56] and once again, 'Your festivals my soul hates'.[57]

You have gathered here, therefore, my beloved, to commemorate today this blessed and holy champion and patron, Saint Abba Onnophrius the blessed anchorite, my beloved children, for it is a very necessary thing, and a thing of great and good renown,[58] to commemorate the righteous one. Above all, walk in all godliness and all wisdom, which are in Christ Jesus our Lord, as I have already said, giving glory to God and glorifying all the virtues of the righteous one, and honoring the priests of God and the servants of the holy altar.

First of all, when you wish to leave your homes to come to the feast, first pray while you are still in your homes, asking the Lord in prayer to make straight your path;[59] in addition, continue to say the words of God and speak of the contests and way of life of the saints. Do not have anything to do with the foolish, whom I have already spoken to you about, that is, with singing and clapping your hands, which you are accustomed to doing, you dissolute women, and the fairy tales that you sing, these so-called 'laments'. Furthermore, when you arrive at the *martyrion* of the saints, go straight to the church. Pray and beseech the righteous saint to enable you to do the things that are pleasing to him in your life. Then, beseech the righteous saint, Abba Onnophrius, to intercede for you before the Lord, that he make you worthy to inherit heaven with him, and be eager diligently to keep vigil, fighting against drowsiness by saying holy psalms and giving the responses to those who are singing psalms, paying attention and with no one speaking any idle words to his neighbor in church. Furthermore, do not leave the church to sit by the door and speak vain and empty words to one another in whispered conversation, for in doing so you are despising the word of

---

[55]Am 5:21.
[56]Am 5:22.
[57]Is 1:14.
[58]Many in Pisentius' congregation would have appreciated the connection between 'good' (*nouf*) and Onnophrius (*ouanofre*); see n. 13.
[59]See Prv 3:6 and Mt 3:3.

God and honoring distracting and idle chatter more than the holy word of God. Instead, be especially attentive to what is read to you in church, and place these words in your heart so you may continue to say them in your homes with your children and your neighbors at all times.

Thus when you finish the night vigil in this way, with an understanding befitting the saints, be careful not to taste any food; do not drink or eat anything at all until you have received Communion and heard the deacon say 'Go in peace'. Moreover, there is this other important requirement: very carefully watch yourself when you are approaching the altar, with great circumspection; do not be in haste as you walk, but walk in an orderly manner. After you have received Communion and heard the deacon say 'Go in peace', when you return home with your children, do not eat or drink excessively, but give your body what it needs. Take care, also, my beloved children, to give to the poor a portion of your bread, your food and your wine, that the Lord may bless you and the things you eat, since through all of them you have first given to God. For it is He who said, 'Whoever gives a drink to one of these little ones, even a cup of cold water, in the name of a disciple, will not lose his reward'.[60] And when you eat, eat in the fear of God, not insatiably, but with reverence and moderation;[61] not with drunkenness but with joy and gladness, saying the psalms with all your heart and blessing God.[62] Let the word of God be in your mouths together with your food. Just as it is necessary to make use of food for the body, it is even more necessary to provide the soul with spiritual food, that is, the word of God. Take care, therefore, that, while you eat the food of this world for your body, you also nourish the soul with the things of God, for the food of the soul is the word of God. Indeed, food for the body must be bought with money, and temptations are inevitable until you collect the money for your needs, but the food of the soul is the word of God: you find it *gratis*, without temptation.

---

[60]Mt 10:12.
[61]Literally: being filled, satisfied (*cei*); 'insatiably' renders the negative of *cei*.
[62]Eph 5:19.

When you finish doing all the appropriate things for the holy feast days and you return to your homes in peace, do not stop meditating at all times on the word of Christ, who has given power to the righteous and all the martyrs, and continue [praying][63] day and night so that you may be worthy to share in the inheritance with the saints.[64] Thus holy scripture has commanded us: 'Remember the Lord and you will accomplish everything I wish'.[65] With regard to ourselves, if the remembrance of the saint abides in our souls at all times, we will say with the holy psalmist David, each one of us: 'I have kept the Lord before me at all times. Because he is at my right hand, I shall not be moved; my flesh will yet live in hope'.[66] The 'movement' of which he speaks is the inclination toward sin. If a person places God before him at all times, and fixes on Him the eyes of the soul and abides with Him, he will never incline toward sin. This, then, is the thought on which all the saints reflect[67] until they attain the measure of perfection. Brothers and my beloved children, let us, too, keep our passage from this temporary dwelling place before our eyes at all times and thus let us refrain from sin. For truly we do not know the day or the hour in which we will be taken, whether we are willing or not, from this temporary dwelling place, to which we shall be forever strangers.[68] Meditating on death, then, will cause us to flee from sin. For this reason I exhort you to remove yourselves from sin.

If my words have saddened some of you, I can nevertheless not remain silent and not speak to you about your salvation. My heart is more than a little heavy when I see the trouble that afflicts you. I very much tremble for you if you are *not* afraid! How can you be so completely unaware that I am afraid for you? For you have seen the great and numerous diseases that God has often brought upon us on account of our sins. For holy scripture says: 'Do not do like the Gentiles'.[69] It

---

[63]Crum suggests, 53 n. 2, that a word has dropped out.
[64]Col 1:12.
[65]Crum could not identify this quotation, and neither can I.
[66]See Ps 16:8–9.
[67]Gk: *philosophia*, interestingly. Crum suggests it should read *philosophei*.
[68]See Lk 12:16–21 and Mt 24:36.
[69]See Mt 6:7–8.

is for this reason that I want you to turn from your sins, each person according to his nature.⁷⁰ Perhaps God will have mercy because we have turned away from sin and will stop being angry with us, for he has prepared his mercy for those who turn away from their sins and produce fruits worthy of repentance.⁷¹ Indeed, it is God who has spoken through the prophet Ezekiel: 'The wickedness of the wicked will not humiliate him on the day that he turns from his wickedness'.⁷² But if we do not turn from our sins at all, he will sharpen his sword as he has sharpened it for others.⁷³ Furthermore, they have often added day to day, remaining in their sins, and now that terrible hour has come upon them without their knowing it; they do not realize that they have become food for the fire and the worm for ever.⁷⁴ Woe to those who have no concern for their own salvation and who continue to remain in their sins until they die!

Men, who has stopped you from taking a woman so that you cease from fornicating? Or women, who is it that has stopped you from taking a man according to the law so that you might not find any pretext for fornication?⁷⁵ If it is impossible for you to practice abstinence, look! Pure marriage has been permitted for us: take a woman to yourself according to the law, and let the woman also take a man, so that sin does not take *you*. Only, do not fornicate,⁷⁶ for in your wretched condition you are not able to bear punishment, you who defile your bodies in fornication, whether you are men or women. If you see an axe or sword about to cut into your body or your flesh, fear and trembling will almost make you freeze like a rock, and you will fervently and tearfully beg, while you confess and promise those who are punishing you that you will not sin any more. If, then, you have been afraid

---

⁷⁰Or, as Crum suggests, 64 n. 3, 'each according to the type (of sin he has committed)'.
⁷¹Mt 3:8.
⁷²Ez 33:12.
⁷³See Ez 21:11. Crum notes, 65 n. 6, that Shenoute 'composed one of his most remarkable homilies on this theme'.
⁷⁴See Mk 9:48 (Is 66:24).
⁷⁵See 1 Cor 7:9.
⁷⁶See 1 Cor 7:28.

of those who punish you concerning the destruction of your body, which you deserve, you wretch, when will you fear God, who has the power to destroy both your soul and your body in Gehenna[77] because you have not removed yourself from sin? For you hear the judgement upon you all the time, you fornicator, as God says to you, 'Whoever defiles God's temple, God will destroy that person'.[78] And again you have heard concerning those who sin that 'their flesh will fall off while they still stand on their feet, and their eyes will become blind in their sockets, and their tongues will turn gangrenous in their mouths',[79] and again, <Their>[80] 'worm will not die and their fire will not be extinguished, and all flesh will see them'.[81]

My brothers, let us flee God's anger, and let us fear him. Let us, moreover, fear our evil ways and impure passions, which have become inseparable from us, so that we too may say with assurance, 'I will leap over a wall'[82]—I mean the wall of the passions that encircles us, that is, our own sins. Yes, I exhort you, do not listen to these words only to discard them behind you;[83] do not leave them in the church where they were read to you, emptied of their power, while you leave. No, let us <write> them on the <tablets> of our heart;[84] let us say them at all times in our homes and on the streets and while we are walking on the road, even while we are eating [or] drinking, even when we are doing work with our hands. Let us recite them to our wives and our[85] children and our servants and our apprentices[86] and <those whom> we hire. They will ask us about them, and <we>

---

[77]Mt 10:28.
[78]See 1 Cor 3:17. Pisentius has changed Paul's 'Whoever destroys' to 'Whoever defiles'.
[79]Zec 14:12.
[80]Reading with Crum *mpeubnt* for *mpenbnt*.
[81]Is 66:24.
[82]Ps 18:29.
[83]See Ps 50:17.
[84]See Prv 3:3, 7:3.
[85]Text: their.
[86]Or: pupils.

must... them... on the day of judgement.[87] Heaven forbid that the occasion should arise where it is said that not only did we <not> heed such words to stop sinning, but we also tolerated others who were sinning and did not rebuke them! No, let us also be able to say with assurance, 'I will tell your name to my brothers',[88] <and again,> 'I have <treasured your word> in my heart',[89] and again, 'I did not lose a single one of those whom you gave me'.[90]

God, who loves us, whose desire is to have compassion,[91] who does not want anyone to perish,[92] but who forgets our wickedness and disregards the things we have done that grieve him, has reined in his anger in order not to explode over our wretchedness; he has made us worthy of his great mercy and has enabled us to set ourselves upright from all our filthiness and sin, that we may be made clean for him, a holy nation and people worthy of life.[93] In pardoning us especially for all our past carelessness and indifference,[94] he has dissolved the enmity that we have caused between us and him and reconciled us again and saved us from our wretchedness; he has given <us> the grace of his mercy on the day of our necessity, through the prayers and intercessions of all <our> holy fathers who from the beginning of this age have been pleasing to him, and especially Saint Abba Onnophrius the anchorite, at <whose holy shrine> we are gathered <today> as <we celebrate his> holy <feast day>... and our Lord Jesus Christ's love for us, through whom is the glory of the Father with him and the Holy Spirit, life-giver and consubstantial, now and always for all ages of ages. Amen.

The discourse is now finished that Abba Pisentius proclaimed on the mountain of Tsinti[95] concerning Abba Onnop-

---

[87]There was probably here something like 'we must be accountable for them on the day of judgement'.
[88]Ps 22:22.
[89]Ps 119:11. This is my conjecture.
[90]Jn 18:9.
[91]Or: mercy, and throughout; Coptic *na*. See Is 54:8.
[92]2 Peter 3:9.
[93]See 1 Pt 2:9 (Ex 19:6).
[94]See n. 37 above.
[95]'Mountain', Coptic *toou*, often indicates a monastic community. On Tsinti (or Tsenti, modern el-Asas), see Wolfgang Kosack, *Historisches Kartenwerk Ägyptens*

hrius, to the glory of God.

God, who accepted the sacrifice of Abel[96] and the two small coins from the widow,[97] likewise, Lord, bless him who has had the care of this work,[98] a commemoration of Saint Abba Onnophrius, so that he may receive favor before God and that God may grant the forgiveness of his sins. Amen.

May Christ also watch over the life of the all-virtuous and [spirit-bearing father]...of the city of Keft...holy...over us. <Amen.>

<Written> in the year of the Martyrs 748, the year of the <Saracens>, 422.[99]

Remember me in love, me Shenoute. Pray for us that he may have mercy on us. Amen.

(Bonn: Rudolf Habelt, 1971) 33, 40; and 'Karten des koptischen Ägypten' 8n (grid number).

[96] See Gn 4:4.
[97] See Lk 21:1–4.
[98] Literally: book; originally a roll or scroll.
[99] That is, 1031–32 AD.

BIBLIOGRAPHY

Adams, William Y. *Nubia: Corridor to Africa*. Princeton 1977.
———. 'Post Pharaonic Nubia in the Light of Archaeology I.' *Journal of Egyptian Archaeology* 50 (1964) 102–120.
———. 'Post Pharaonic Nubia in the Light of Archaeology II.' *Journal of Egyptian Archaeology* 51 (1965) 160–178.
———. 'Post Pharaonic Nubia in the Light of Archaeology III.' *Journal of Egyptian Archaeology* 52 (1966) 147–162.
Amélineau, E. *La géographie de l'Égypt à l'époque copte*. Paris 1893.
———. 'Voyage d'un moine Egyptien dans le desert.' *Recueil de trauvaux relatifs a la philologie et a l'archéologie* 6 (1885) 166–194.
Anderson, Robert and Ibrahim Fawzy. *Egypt Revealed: Scenes from Napoleon's Description de l'Egypt*. Cairo 1987.
Baedeker, Karl. *Egypt and the Sudan*. New York 1929.
Balestri, I., ed. and H. Hyvernat. *Acta Martyrum* I (*Corpus Scriptorum Christianorum Orientalium* v. 43–44; *Scriptores Coptici* v. 3–4). Louvain 1955.
Bell, H. Idris. *Jews and Christians in Egypt*. London 1924.
Blackman, Winifred S. *The Fellāhīn of Upper Egypt: Their Religious, Social, and Industrial Life To-day, with Special Reference to Survivals from Ancient Times*. London, 1927.
Bouyer, Louis. *Cosmos*. Petersham, Mass. 1988.
———. *Spirituality of the New Testament and the Fathers*. A History of Christian Spirituality 1. [New York-London], repr. Minneapolis, Minn. 1963.
Bowman, Alan K. *Egypt After the Pharoahs: 332 BC–AD 642 from Alexander to the Arab Conquest*. [London] 1986.
Brown, Peter. *The Body and Society: Men, Women and Sexual Renunciation in Early Christianity*. New York 1988.

Brunner, Hellmut. 'Eine altägyptische Idealbiographie in christlichem Gewande.' *Zeitschrift für Ägyptische Sprache und Altertumskunde* 99.Ib (1973) 88–94.

Budge, E.A. Wallis. *Coptic Martyrdoms Etc. in the Dialect of Upper Egypt. Coptic Texts*, vol. IV. New York 1977 (London 1914).

———. *Miscellaneous Coptic Texts. Coptic Texts*, vol. V, parts 1 & 2, New York 1977 (London 1915).

———. *The Paradise or Garden of the Holy Fathers.* . . . London 1907.

Butler, Dom Cuthbert. *The Lausiac History of Palladius.* London 1898.

Cadell, H. and R. Rémondon. 'Sens et emplois de τὸ ὄρος dans les documents papyrologiques.' *Revue des études grecques* 80 (1967) 343–349.

Cassian, John. *Conferences*, tr. by Colm Luibheid. New York 1985.

Chadwick, Owen. *John Cassian.* London 1968.

Chauler, D. Sylvestre. 'Saint Onuphre.' *Les Cahiers Coptes* 5 (1954) 3–15.

Chitty, Derwas J. *The Desert A City.* Crestwood, New York n.d.

Coquin, René-Georges. 'Onophrius, Saint.' *The Coptic Encyclopaedia.* New York 1991: vol. 6: pp. 1841–2.

———. 'Paphnutius the Hermit, Saint.' *The Coptic Encyclopaedia.* New York 1991: vol. 6: pp. 1882–3.

Cross, F.L. and E.A. Livingstone. *The Oxford Dictionary of the Christian Church.* 2nd Ed., Oxford 1983.

Crum, W.E. *A Coptic Dictionary.* Oxford 1979 [1939].

———. 'Discours de Pisenthius sur Saint Onnophrius.' *Revue de l'Orient Chrétien*, 2nd series 10 (20) (1915–1917) 38–67.

Delehaye, Hippolytus. 'Les martyrs d'Égypte,' (Appendice I: La passion de S. Paphnuce). *Analecta Bollandiana* 40 (1922) 328–343.

Emery, W.B. *Egypt in Nubia.* London 1965.

Evelyn White, Hugh G. *The Monasteries of the Wâdi 'N Natrûn.* New York 1926–1933 (repr. 1973).

Evetts, B.T.A. and Alfred J. Butler. *The Churches and Monasteries of Egypt and Some Neighbouring Countries. Attributed to Abû Ṣâliḥ, the Armenian.* London 1969 (Oxford 1895)

Festugière, A.-J., ed. *Historia Monachorum in Aegypto* (*Subsidia Hagiographica* no. 34). Brussels 1961.

Gillispie, Charles Coulston and Michel Dewachter. *Monuments of Egypt: The Napoleonic Edition. The Complete Archaelogical Plates from La Description de l'Egypte*. Princeton 1987.

Griggs, C. Wilfred. *Early Egyptian Christianity from its Origins to 451 C.E.* Coptic Studies 2; Leiden 1990.

Guy, Jean-Claude, ed. *Jean Cassien: Institutions Cénobitiques*. Sources Chretiennes 109. Paris 1965.

Harvey, Paul B. 'Jerome: Life of Paul, the First Hermit', in Vincent L. Wimbush, ed., *Ascetic Behavior in Greco-Roman Antiquity: A Sourcebook*. Minneapolis, 1990, pp. 357–69.

Haycock, Bryan G. 'The Later Phases of Meroitic Civilization.' *Journal of Egyptian Archaeology* 53 (1967) 107–120.

Hobbs, A. Hoyt and Joy Adzigian. *Fielding's Egypt and the Archaeological Sites*. New York 1984.

Jones, A.H.M. *The Later Roman Empire 284–602*. Baltimore 1986

Judge, E.A. 'The Earliest Use of Monachos for "Monk" (P. Coll. Youtie 77) and the Origins of Monasticism.' *Jahrbuch für Antike und Christentum* 20 (1977), 72–89.

Kammerer, Winifred. *A Coptic Bibliography*. New York 1969 (Ann Arbor, Michigan 1950).

Kosack, Wolfgang. *Historisches Kartenwerk Ägyptens*. Bonn 1971.

Lampe, G.W.H. *A Patristic Greek Lexicon*. Oxford 1961.

Layton, Bentley. *Catalogue of Coptic Literary Manuscripts in the British Library Acquired Since the Year 1906*. London 1987.

Leclercq, H. 'Paphnuce.' *Dictionnaire d'archéologie chrétienne et de liturgie* v. 13.1, 1358–1361.

———. 'Philae.' *Dictionnaire d'archéologie chrétienne et de liturgie* v. 14.1, 692–703.

Lefort, L.Th. 'Fragments Coptes.' *Le Muséon* 58 (1945) 97–120.

———, ed. *S. Pachomii vita Bohairice scripta. Corpus Scriptorum Christianorum Orientalium* 89, *Scriptores Coptici* 7. Louvain 1953.

Liddell, Henry George and Robert Scott. *A Greek-English Lexicon*. Oxford, 1968.

Lyons, H.G. *A Report on the Temples of Philae*. Cairo 1908.

MacQuitty, William. *Island of Isis: Philae, Temple of the Nile*. New York 1976.

Martin, Annick. 'Aux origines de l'église copte: L'implantation et le developpemont du christianisme en Égypte (Ie-IVe siècles).' *Revue des études anciennes* 83/1 (1981) 35–56.

Merton, Thomas. *The Wisdom of the Desert Fathers.* New York 1960.

Milne, J. Grafton. *A History of Egypt Under Roman Rule.* London 1924.

Morard, F.-E. 'Monachos, moine. Histoire du terme grec jusq'au 4e siècle.' *Freiburger Zeitschrift für Philosophie und Theologie* 20 (1973) 332–411.

Munier, H. 'Le Christianisme a Philae.' *Bulletin de la société d'archéologie Copte* 4 (1938) 37–49.

O'Leary, De Lacy. *The Saints of Egypt.* London and New York 1937.

Orlandi, Tito. *Koptische Papyri Theologischen Inhalts. Mitteilungen aus der Papyrussamlung der Österreichische Nationalbibliothek* n.s. v.9. Wien 1974.

Palladius. *The Lausiac History*, translated and annotated by Robert T. Meyer. New York 1964.

Pearson, Birger A. and James E. Goehring, eds., *The Roots of Egyptian Christianity.* Studies in Antiquity and Christianity 1; Philadelphia 1986.

Pieper, Karl. *Atlas Orbis Christiani Antiqui.* Düsseldorf 1931.

Rémondon, Roger. 'L'Égypte et la suprême resistance au christianisme.' *Bulletin de l'Insitut Français d'Archéologie Orientale du Caire* 51 (1952) 63–78.

Rubenson, Samuel. *The Letters of St. Antony: Origenist Theology, Monastic Tradition and the Making of a Saint.* Lund 1990.

Russell, Norman, tr. *The Lives of the Desert Fathers.* Kalamazoo, London, Oxford 1981.

Shinnie, P.L. *Medieval Nubia* (Sudan Antiquities Service: Museum Pamphlet No. 2). Khartoum, 1954.

Skeat, T.C. 'A Letter from the King of the Blemmyes to the King of the Noubades.' *Journal of Egyptian Archaeology* 63 (1977) 159–170.

Spiegelberg, Wilhelm. 'Der Falkenkultus auf der Insel Philae in christlicher Zeit.' *Archiv für Papyrusforschung und verwandte Gebiete* 7 (1924) 186–189.

Theodoret of Cyrrhus. *A History of the Monks of Syria*, translated with an introduction and notes by R.M. Price. Kalamazoo, Michigan 1985.

Till, Walter. *Koptischen Heiligen- und Martyerlegenden*, Erster Teil. *Orientalia Christiana Analecta* 102, 14–19.

Veilleux, Armand. *La liturgie dans le cénobitisme Pachômien au quatrième siècle*. Rome 1968.

———. 'Monasticism and Gnosis in Egypt,' in Birger A. Pearson and James E. Goehring, eds., *The Roots of Egyptian Christianity*, pp. 271–306. Philadelphia 1986.

———, tr. *Pachomian Koinonia*. Vol. 1, *The Life of Saint Pachomius and his Disciples*. Kalamazoo, Michigan 1980.

Vivian, Tim. 'Journeying into God: The Story of Abba Pambo.' *Cistercian Studies Quarterly* 26:2 (1991), 95–106.

———. '*The Life of Onnophrius*: A New Translation', *Coptic Church Review* 12:4 (Winter 1991) 99–111.

———. *Saint Peter of Alexandria: Bishop and Martyr*. Philadelphia, 1988.

Ward, Benedicta, tr. *The Sayings of the Desert Fathers: The Alphabetical Collection*. Kalamazoo, Michigan 1984.

Wilcken, Ulrich. 'Heidnisches und Christliches aus Ägypten. I: Das Christentum auf der Insel Philae.' *Archiv für Papyrusforschung und verwandte Gebiete* 1 (1901) 396–407.

Wimbush, Vincent L., ed. *Ascetic Behavior in Greco-Roman Antiquity: A Sourcebook*. Minneapolis 1990.

Wipszycka, Ewa. 'La christianisation de l'Égypte aux IVe-VIe siècles. Aspects sociaux et ethniques.' *Aegyptus* 68 (1988) 142–58.

Winkelmann, F. 'Paphnutios, der Bekenner und Bischof.' *Probleme der koptischen Literatur*, ed. by Peter Nagel. Halle 1968. Pp. 145–53.

Winlock, H.E. and W.E. Crum. *The Monastery of Epiphanius at Thebes*. New York 1926.

Witt, R. E. *Isis in the Graeco-Roman World*. London 1971.

Zabkar, L.V. 'Adaptation of Ancient Egyptian Texts to the Temple Ritual at Philae.' *Journal of Egyptian Archaeology* 66 (1980), 127–136.

SCRIPTURE INDEX

HEBREW SCRIPTURES

Genesis	
17:4	101
17:19	134
18:10	134
24:33	73
24:54	73
28:12	138
30:22–24	134

Exodus	
17:6	138
17:11–13	81
17:12	81
20:17	127
20:26	144

Leviticus	
18:6ff.	144

Numbers	
20:11	151

Deuteronomy	
5:21	127
13:14	144

1 Samuel	
2:21	
17:36	115

Judges	
15:19	138

1 Kings	
21:13–19	127
22:34–38	127

2 Kings	
3:11	84
5:27	125

Psalms	
9:9–12(?)	151
12:5	136
22:25	102
30:11	81
34:6	151
34:6(?)	136
60:12	119
68:1	119
68:13	76
69:33	136
83:1(LXX)	73
119:103	77

Isaiah	
5:8	127
40:30(LXX)	151
42:3	104

195

48:21	151	Micah	
64:4	82	2:2	127
65:8	104		

CHRISTIAN SCRIPTURES

Matthew
3:4	76
4:4	154
5:4	81
5:7	127
5:8	76
5:13	77
5:28	74
6:6	103
6:14	96, 127
6:24	74
6:29	114
6:31–33	154
8:12	82, 147 n. 19
8:22	75
9:48	147 n. 19
10:9	136
10:12–13	73
10:16	77
10:23	89
10:28	89
10:37–38	78, 116
10:39	79
10:42	138
11:11	150
11:28	117, 131
15:26–28	102
16:26	79
18:6	138
18:10	138
18:14	138
18:28	129
25:14–23	129
25:34	131
25:35–36	131
25:41	131

Mark
3:17	103 n. 42
9:41	128
9:48	82

Luke
2:51	86
4:4	154
7:1–10	125
9:62	75
14:13	1387
16:13	74
16:19–31	127 n. 68

John
5:14	148
12:25	79
14:12	35, 130
21:6	131

Acts
1:21–26	98
2:17	91
6:3	98
8:20	125
10:9–28	102
10:24–28	101 n. 41
13:11	89

Romans
3:29–30	101

1 Corinthians
2:9	82
3:6	78

2 Corinthians
2:12–13   78

Galatians
2:10   40

Ephesians
6:12   83

1 Thessalonians
2:9   130
5:17   102

2 Timothy
2:4–5   75

Hebrews
12:22–23   82

James
1:15   74, 146
1:26   102
2:13   127, 138
5:16   82

1 Peter
2:12   119
4:8   104
5:8   77

Revelation
16:15   144

INDEX OF NAMES

Aaron 25, 31–38, 40–1, 51, 53–4, 68–9, 84–5, 87, 114–40.
Abû Ṣâliḥ 20, 57, 61.
Agenios 20
Anianus 78–9, 82–3.
Anthony 20, 22, 33, 53.
Aphraates 35.
Apollo (monk) 20, 31, 66–7.
Appion 63–4, 66, 68.
Aswan 20, 50, 53, 54, 54–69, 78, 85–6, 109, 125.
Athanasius 43, 52, 55, 64–5, 86–7, 99–105, 111 n.54.

Banouphiel 83.
Blemmyes 58, 59 n.134, 60.

Cassian 27 n.29, 44, 47–9, 53, 111 n.53, 111 n.54.
Christ 33–6, 38, 78, 81, 127–8, 131, 133–5, 137–8.

Diocletian 43, 55, 58, 59 n.135, 61.

Elephantine 57–8, 62.
Elias 21–3.
Epiphanius 43, 43 n.68.

Gelasius 43 n.68.

Helle 28.
Hierasykaminos 58.

Historia Monachorum 20 n.10, 21, 22 n.18, 23, 23 n.22, 24, 28, 30 n.37, 31 n.40, 36 n.46, 41, 45, 53, 61–2, 66, 158 n.42.
Histories of the Monks of Upper Egypt 17–18, 25, 30–1, 38, 42–3, 46, 50–4, 64–6, 69–70, 72–140.

Isaac 25, 33, 37–8, 40–1, 50, 64, 69, 84–5, 116–19, 140.
Isaiah 52–3, 88–92, 96, 98, 108–10.
Isis 59–60, 62, 65, 67.

Jerome 22 n.21, 158 n.42.
Jesus (see Christ)
Jews 157.
John 75–8.
John of Lycopolis 23, 28, 36.
Juvenal 58.
Justinian 60, 62.

Life of Onnophrius 17–18, 25–6, 28–9, 29 n.35, 30 n.36, 38–9, 42–3, 46, 50, 52–3, 55, 69–70, 142–64.
Life of Pachomius 21, 36, 39 n.53, 42 n.60, 55, 99 n.36, 111 n.53, 111 n. 54, 137 n.73.

Macarius of Alexandria 44.
Macarius of Egypt 44.
Macedonius 32, 52–4, 64–6, 85–99, 107–8, 110.

Mark 52–3, 65–6, 88–108, 110.
Matthew 80.
Merton, Thomas 18, 18 n.3, 18 n.4, 23 n.23, 26.

Nile 19, 31–2, 57, 88, 136–8.
Nineveh 127.
Nitria 28.
Nobadae 58, 60.
Nubia, Nubians 25, 32, 35, 57–8, 60, 92–4, 101, 118, 120–1.

Onnophrius 22, 25–6, 39–40, 149–64.
Or 20 n.10.
Origen 23, 41.

Pachomius 21 n.15, 21 n.16, 21 n.17, 27 n.28, 27 n.29, 36, 38 n.51, 39– 40.
Palamon 21, 40.
Palladius 44, 46, 48–9, 53, 111 n.53.
Pambo 24–5, 41.
Paphnutius 24, 26, 29–30, 33, 36, 38–41, 42–50, 50–54, 64–9, 73–140, 142–64; Paphnutius Bubalis 46–50, 53; Paphnutius Cephalas 45–7, 51 n.109, 53.
Paul (monk) 78–9, 82–3.
Paul (Jerome's *Life of Paul*) 158 n.42, 160 n.44.

Philae 30, 32, 50–54, 54–69, 106, 114, 123, 140.
Phou-p-koht 103.
Pseleusias 52–3, 65, 110–14.
Pseleusius 50, 73–7, 84.

Rome, Romans 57–60.

Saba 27.
Serapamon 79–80.
Scetis 47–9, 53, 164.
Schissa (Schedia) 105.
Shmoun 150.
Shenoute 66.
Strabo 67–8.
Sulūh 31, 92 n.29a.
Syncletica (of Palestine) 22 n.20.

Theodore 36.
Theodore, bp. of Philae 62.
Theodoret of Cyrrhus 36 n.44, 113 n.55.
Theodosius 63.
Theophilus, bp. of Alexandria 48, 52, 65–6, 113.
Timothy (monk) 39, 144–49.
Timothy, bp. of Alexandria 52, 113.

Wadi Natrun (see Scetis).

Zacchaeus (monk) 79, 80–3.
Zebulon (monk) 77–8.

INDEX OF SUBJECTS

anchorites 13, 41, 151.
angels 18, 24, 26, 40, 157, 162–3.
amthropomorphism 48.
Apophthegmata 41, 44, 54, 143 n. 3, 150 n. 23.
apotaktikoi (monks) 22 n. 21.
ascesis 24, 29, 38–40, 118–20, 136, 153, 162.

baptism 34, 51.

cenobites 13, 41.
Communion (see eucharist).

demons 33, 79, 119–20, 134–5.
desert 18–26, 78, 143, 147, 149–50, 153.
Devil 29, 38, 118, 120, 146–7.

eucharist 26–30, 38, 83, 92, 107, 109, 112, 154, 162.

falcon (idol) 65–7, 87–8.

fasting 39.

hesychia 39, 39 n. 52, 40, 145.
holy men and women 30–7, 40, 92 n. 29a, 110–14, 114–40.
hospitality 29, 39.

manuscripts 69–70.
miracles 26, 29, 32, 120–39.
monastery 20, 83.
mountain 18–26, 150, 155.
mystery 30.

nun (*monachē*) 13 n. 1, 146 n. 16, 146–7.

politeia 17–18, 33, 143, 151, 154.
phrourion (fort) 63–64.
prayer 39, 126, 131, 162.
psalms, psalter 20.

spirituality 17–41.
synaxis 26–30, 150.

INDEX TO PISENTIUS' *DISCOURSE*

Abel 188

Christ 175, 176, 181, 182, 184, 187, 188
    word of Christ 176, 184
Christians 181
Communion 183

daughters 181
David 177, 184
distractions 181

Eli 181
Ezekiel 185

faith 176
fasts 178
Father (God) 187
fornication 185

God 175, 176, 178, 181, 182, 183, 184, 185, 186, 187, 188
    God's anger 186, 187
    God's compassion 187
    God's law 175
    God's mercy 187
    word of God 175, 182–83, 183

husband 176
Holy Spirit 187

judgement 187

Keft 175, 188
kingdom of heaven 179, 180

Lent 178

marriage 176, 178, 185
men 185

neighbor 179

Onnophrius 175, 176, 177, 178, 180, 182, 187, 188
    feast day 178, 187
    way of life 176, 177, 180

patience 177
Paul (apostle) 175
Pisentius 175, 187
pray/prayer 182
purity 176, 178

saints, the 175, 177, 178, 179, 180, 184
Shenoute (scribe) 188
shrine 178, 187
sin 184
sons 181

temptation 183
Tsinti 187

vigils 178, 183

wife/wives 176, 186
woman/women 180, 185
    dissolute women 182

young people 176

ADDITIONS AND CORRECTIONS FOR THE REVISED EDITION

Page 14 n. 2: for 'quotienne' read 'quotidienne'.

Page 18 n. 3: the page numbers for the article 'Reading the Saints' are 17–58.

Page 22 n. 20: for the article 'Syncletica' see now Tim Vivian, *Journeying into God: Seven Early Monastic Lives* (Minneapolis: Fortress, 1996) 37–52.

Page 25 n. 25: for the story of Abba Pambo see now Vivian, *Journeying*, 25–36.

Page 67 n. 171. On late paganism in Egypt and on Philae, see Lásló Kákosy, 'Das Ende des Heidentums in Ägypten' and Adelheid Burkhardt, 'Zu späten heidnischen Priestern in Philae', in Peter Nagel, ed., *Graeco-Coptica: Griechen und Kopten im byzantinischen Ägypten* (Halle/Salle: Martin-Luther Universität, 1984) 61–76 and 77–83.

Page 70 n. 178: for 'Paphnutius' read 'Onnophrius'.

Page 70 n. 178: for the revised edition I have added a translation of Pisentius' 'Discourse on Saint Onnophrius'. See the Appendix, pp. 167–188.

Page 99, par. 56, line 16: delete 'a' after 'of': 'of such a thing'.

Page 127 n. 68: for the story of Dives and Lazarus in the homily 'On Riches', see Pearson and Vivian, *Two Coptic Homilies* (Rome: Corpus dei Copti Manoscritti Letterari, 1993) 104–107. A thirteenth-century depiction of Dives in hell asking Lazarus, who is in the bosom of Abraham in heaven, for a drop of water can now be seen in the Old Church at the Monastery of Saint Antony by the Red Sea.

Page 146 n. 10: for a striking pictorial image of Saint Onnophrius from the monastery of Saint Macarius in the Wadi Natrun (Scetis), one that corresponds to the descriptions here of Timothy and Onnophrius, see Nabil Selim Atalla, *Coptic Art: Wallpaintings* (Cairo: Lehnert and Landrock, n.d.) 82.